GACE

Early Childhood Quick Review

Parts 001 & 002

For Reference Not to be taken from this library

Andrea Browning

Thomas University Library
1501 Millpond Road
Thomasville, GA 31792

First Edition

© Copyright 2011

DISCLOSURE: This book is not representative of, or affiliated with, the Georgia Department of Education or Georgia Assessment of Certified Educators in any way.

The Early Childhood GACE Consists of Two Exams
Test Codes 001 and 002

Introduction: When I set out to study for the Early Childhood GACE, I was very disappointed to find that the available resources were very limited and had poor reviews. So I decided I would create my own using the frameworks available from the GACE website. To find the relevant information for each of the frameworks, I bought several textbooks. Once I was finished, I had a good study manual that covered both of the Early Childhood Exams (001 and 002).

IMPORTANT: Of course there is going to be much more information in this study manual than actually appears in the exam. It is your job to read through the provided information and learn the Big Ideas and not get bogged down in the details.

DISCLOSURE: This book is not representative of, or affiliated with, the Georgia Department of Education or Georgia Assessment of Certified Educators in any way.

Design of this Text

This text is organized according to the test frameworks provided by the GACE website. There is a link located on the GACE website, www.gace.nesinc.com, for the frameworks, as well as practice questions. The practice questions seem to be good representations of the types of questions that will be found in the exam, though there is only a very small sample.

DISCLOSURE: This book is not representative of, or affiliated with, the Georgia Department of Education or the Georgia Assessment of Certified Educators in any way.

Table of Contents

Suggestions Related to GACE: 7
Random Facts and Suggestions: 8
Strategies: 8
Design of Exam 9
How to Use this Book: 10

PART 1 Test 1 (Test Code 001) 11
Reading, English, and Language Arts 13
    Phonological Awareness 14
    Phonics 20
    Vocabulary 26
    Fluency and Comprehension 31
    Informational Texts and Literature 36
    Writing 44
    English Grammar 50
    Reading and Writing across the Curriculum 56

Social Studies: 59
    Georgia, U.S., and World History Events 60
    Geography 78
    Government and Civics 84
    Economics 88

Table of Contents

PART 2 Test 2 (Test Code 002) 93

Mathematics 95

    Exploring Mathematics and Solving Problems 97

    Numbers and Mathematical Operations 100

    Geometry 119

    Algebra 127

    Data Analysis 137

    Answers and Solution for Math Review 142

Science 153

    Characteristics and Processes of Science 154

    Earth Science 160

    Physical Science 177

    Life Science 188

Heath, Physical Education, and the Arts 197

    Health and Safety 198

    Physical Education 206

    The Arts 209

Math Review Questions 213

Math Review Answers 229

Suggestions Related to GACE:

- Bring your admission ticket; it contains your test code information, test time, and seat number.

- Be sure to bring two forms of identification, one of which must be a picture ID. The information must be in English.

- In most locations, if not all, seating is assigned.

- Get to the testing site early to find parking and to leave allowances for traffic and finding the testing site. You do not need any more stress on test day, so arrive at least 30 minutes early.

- If you have more than 50 miles to travel, consider staying in a motel.

- The test is approximately four hours long.

- Cell phones will not be permitted in the testing area. The best option is to simply leave it in your car.

- Study – I suggest you take at least a month to prepare for the exam so you are not overwhelmed by the information the night or day before.

- Things not to bring to the testing site: cell phones, MP3 players, scratch paper, books of any kind, calculators, food or drink, and your family and friends.

Random Facts and Suggestions:

- Rest – Be sure to get plenty of rest the night before because you are going to be sitting in a room for up to four hours.

- Eat – As stated previously, you will be in the exam room for a long time, and you will want to focus on the exam, not your rumbling stomach.

- Bring a Jacket – No matter what, especially for summer exam takers.

- Be Prepared – Bring your pencils and plenty of them; no calculators for this exam.

- Focus – It is important to stay on task for this exam.

Strategies:

This would not be a test prep book without a few test-taking strategies. These are simply a review. You did not make it this far without having the ability to take a standardized test.

- ✓ Start by scanning the questions.
  - Answer the easy questions first. These are the questions you can answer right away without hesitation.

- ✓ Next, complete the harder questions.
  - Start by eliminating the answers you know are wrong.
  - You can write on the exam, so cross out the ones you think are wrong.

- ✓ If there is time, be sure to go over your responses to ensure you have answered all of the questions to the best of your ability; however, this is not a time to start second-guessing yourself. Your first choice is usually the best choice.

- ✓ Be sure you answer **all** of the questions.

Design of Exam

This is available for everyone free on the official GACE website:
http://www.gace.nesinc.com/GA_PG_001002_opener.asp

Test I (Test Code 001)

Subareas:	Objectives	Approximate Number of Selected-Response Questions	Constructed-Response Assignments
➢ Reading and English Language Arts	0001–0008	40	1
➢ Social Studies	0009–0012	20	1
	TOTAL	60	2
	Percentage of Test Score	80%	20%

Test II (Test Code 002)

Subareas:	Objectives	Approximate Number of Selected-Response Questions	Constructed-Response Assignments
➢ Mathematics	0013–0017	25	1
➢ Science	0018–0021	20	1
➢ Health, Physical Education, and the Arts	0022–0024	15	
	TOTAL	60	2
	Percentage of Test Score	80%	20%

Copyright © 2008 by the Georgia Professional Standards Commission
Georgia Assessments for the Certification of Educators, GACE, and the GACE logo are trademarks, in the U.S. and/or other countries, of the Georgia Professional Standards Commission and Pearson Education, Inc. or its affiliate(s).
Pearson and its logo are trademarks in the U.S. and/or other countries of Pearson Education, Inc. or its affiliate(s).

Percentages for Test One:
Reading, English and Language Arts
- 40 multiple choice – 53.3%
- 1 written response – 10%

Social Studies
- 20 multiple choice – 26.7%
- 1 written response – 10%

Percentages for Test Two:
Mathematics
- 25 multiple choice – 33.3%
- 1 written response – 10%

Science
- 20 multiple choice – 26.7%
- 1 written response – 10%

Health, P.E., Arts
- 15 multiple choice – 20%

How to Use this Book:

There are five sections for this test. Within each section, there are 24 main objectives or competencies, with each of those having several sub-objectives. The amount of information that is covered in this review guide is immense.

When studying for the exam, do not focus on the intricate details in the subject areas; instead, simply read through the guide a couple of times. No, this may not be the traditional way to study, but it is the best way to cover a large quantity of information.

Content Specific:
- **Language Arts and Reading** – Pay attention to the concepts and strategies, and be able to apply the information to real-world situations. This is how the practice questions are done in the GACE PDF study manual.
- **Social Science** – This section covers a lot of information. Read through the sections a few times and concentrate on the main events of history.
- **Math** – This section is important for the simple fact that we tend to rely on calculators for even simple math, but they are not permitted for this exam. Because of this, practice questions cover conversions, fractions, decimals, integers, and percent's.
- **Science** – This area is also filled with a lot of information. Be sure to read through and re-familiarize yourself with unfamiliar concepts. According to the GACE test website, there is a formula page provided, but formulas are covered in this book.
- **Music, Arts, Physical Education (PE), and Health** – This area is filled with things that may be very new to you or things that are seemingly common sense. Again, just read through the sections; do not get lost in the vocabulary.

PART 1 Test 1 (Test Code 001)

Reading, English, and Language Arts:

This is the longest section of the exam with 40 multiple choice questions and one written response question. This section alone accounts for over 63% of Test One.

Social Studies:

This section consists of 20 multiple choice questions and one essay question covering history, geography, government, and economics. There is a lot of information, with limited questions.

Reading, English, and Language Arts

This section is organized according to the frameworks available in PDF format from the GACE website, www.gace.nesinc.com. There are eight objectives for this section, making it the longest section in the entire Early Childhood Exam.

Items in this section:
- ☑ Phonological awareness
- ☑ Phonics
- ☑ Vocabulary
- ☑ Fluency and comprehension
- ☑ Informational text and literature
- ☑ Writing
- ☑ English grammar
- ☑ Reading and writing across the curriculum

Phonological Awareness
Recognizing stages in learning to read and write

Stages in Reading

Pre-reading Stage:
Students in pre-K and beginning kindergarten are in this stage. Students understand that reading is a process and a skill that they will have to learn.

Initial Reading or Decoding Stage:
Students in grades K through 2 are in this stage. Students learn to recognize letters and associate letters with sounds.

Students use decoding (sounding out), as well as encoding (putting together), to understand what the word is.

Fluency Stage:
Students in grades 2 through 3 are in this stage. Students gain confidence and start following words with their eyes, rather than their fingers. Students are beginning to read for content and knowledge.

Reading for Learning Stage:
Students in grades 4 through 8 are in this stage. Students use prior knowledge and read for content.

Phonological Awareness
Recognizing stages in learning to read and write

Stages in Writing, from the Georgia Department of Education:

Stage 1: The Emerging Writer
- Little or no development, organization, and/or detail
- Students often draw pictures of the story they are telling
- No consideration for audience
- Reader cannot understand intended message

Stage 2: The Developing Writer
- Shows some topic and or organizational development
- Simple words and sentences
- Little consideration for audience
- Errors make it hard to understand

Stage 3: The Focusing Writer
- Clear topic, little development
- Sense of audience
- Simple vocabulary and sentences
- Errors in flow

Stage 4: The Experimenting Writer
- Clear topic
- Written for someone
- Use of vocabulary and different sentence patterns
- Some errors in flow

Stage 5: The Engaging Writer
- Organized beginning, middle, and end
- Engaging
- Varied vocabulary and sentence patterns
- Errors do not interfere

Stage 6: The Extending Writer
- Full of details and organized
- Engaging
- Creative
- Few errors

Phonological Awareness
Purposes of printed information and strategies for promoting familiarity with print

Purposes of Printed Information – Most students begin school with the knowledge that books contain words, those words tell a story, and, therefore, those words have meaning.

If for some reason students do not have this knowledge, it is quickly discovered as the teacher reads a book aloud on the first day of school, holding it for the students to see.

Students observe the direction of reading as the teacher follows along with her finger and turns the pages.

Exposure – is a good way for students to gain familiarity with text and literature. Students should have access to a classroom library, magazines, alternate text, dictionaries, and a thesaurus.

Phonological Awareness
Knowledge of phonological awareness

Things to Know:
Phoneme – is the smallest unit of sound
Example: *make* has 3 phonemes: /m/ /a/ /k/

Phonological Awareness – is the ability to hear the syllables within a word and segment the individual phonemes within each syllable.

The development of phonological awareness is very important for later use in decoding unfamiliar words, reading fluency, and spelling.

Phonological awareness is sometimes confused with phonics, but it is different because phonics requires students to match letters to sounds, while phonological awareness relates only to the sounds.

Phonological Awareness
Knowledge of phonemic awareness

Phonemic Awareness – is a sub-area of phonological awareness, and is the consciousness of individual sounds in words.

Development of phonemic awareness can aid the development of phonological awareness.

Phonemes – As stated earlier, are individual speech sounds; for example, the word *bake* has four letters, though it only has three phonemes: /b/ /a/ /k/.

Phonemic awareness can be taught through interaction with print and/or segmenting words.

Phonological Awareness
Significance of phonological and phonemic awareness in learning to read

Basically, phonological awareness is a broad topic which encompasses phonemic awareness as a component. These skills are important in the process of learning to read.

How to Analyze Student Reading:
Miscue Analysis – is the process of analyzing the cuing system that the student is using: semantic, syntactic, or graphophonic.

  Semantic Cue – Students gain meaning using their past experience by bringing their background knowledge to a story.

  Syntactic Cue – Students gain meaning using knowledge of how language works.

  Graphophonics Cue – Students' ability to sound out words and recognize them as words not just letters.

**Based on the students' use of these cues, students predict the content of text, confirm or revise their predictions, and reread if needed.

Phonological Awareness

Strategies for promoting students' phonological and phonemic awareness

Ways to Develop Awareness:

- Have Fun with Words – This helps students become more aware of the sounds of language on an abstract level.
- Rhyming – also develops phonological awareness.
- Blending – Students create words by combining word parts. Blending builds on students' ability to rhyme and prepares them for segmenting.
    Example: word that begins with /c/ and rhymes with *hat*.
- Phonemic Blending – Some vowels are difficult to detect because they blend in with the consonant that follows them.
    Example: Say the words – *will, girl, train, drum*, and *dress*. The vowels are almost undetectable and this causes confusion for students. They will spell these words *wll, grl, trn, drm, drss*.
- Beginning Consonant Sounds – noting when two words begin with the same sound.
    Example: dog, dig, date
- Segmenting Words – Only after students have developed some sense of rhyme, blending, and initial sounds can they break words into segments.
    Segmenting: breaking words into sounds; *cat* is /k/ /a/ /t/
- Forming sounds – Being aware of articulation fosters phonological awareness

Phonological Awareness

Questions to Recap:

1. In what reading stage do students use decoding and encoding to understand words?
    a. Pre-Reading Stage
    b. Reading for Learning Stage
    c. Initial Reading Stage
    d. Fluency Stage

2. An Engaging Writer uses _____ vocabulary and sentence patterns.

3. A Phoneme is _____.

4. How many phonemes does the word "green" have?

5. What process is used to analyze the cuing system a student uses?

1.) c 2.) varied 3.) the smallest unit of sound 4.) 4 /g/ /r/ /ee/ /n/ 5.) miscue analysis

Phonics

Apply knowledge of letter combinations of words and the sounds of words

Pre-Alphabetic Stage:
This is the first stage of reading. Children use association and symbols to identify words. A common example is when they see the "Golden Arches" and know the sign is for McDonald's. In this stage, children invent spontaneous spelling, using random letters to represent sounds.

Partial Alphabetic Stage:
This stage is also known as the "letter name stage" – students use letter-sound relationships to read words. As students' progress through this stage, they begin using vowels.

Full Alphabetic Stage:
At this stage, students process all letters in words and begin reading, but reading may be slow. They can blend words like *at* with *cat* or *mat*. They also begin spelling.

Consolidated Alphabetic Stage:
This stage is also known as the within-word-pattern stage, and student's process longer and more complex words.

Graphophonemic:
At this stage, students understand that written words are composed of patterns of letters that represent the sounds of spoken words.

Morphemic Reading:
This is described as the process of identifying words by analyzing meaningful parts of the word such as prefixes and suffixes: un-, re-, -er.

Phonics
Phonics skills to decode unfamiliar words

Phonics – is defined as the study of speech sounds related to reading. These skills are essential for readers. Phonics is teaching students how to connect the sounds of spoken English with letters or groups of letters.
  Examples: The sound /k/ can be represented by c, k, ck, or ch

NOTE: Not all words can be sounded out with phonics. These words must be memorized and are called sight words. Knowing these words increases fluency.

Many words that students read are sight words, meaning there is no need to sound the words out. They recognize these words immediately. We use phonics to sound unfamiliar words out.

How We Read Words:
- Predicting (context clues)
- Sound out (letter by letter)
- Chucked (grouping sounds together)
- By analogy (relating letter groups, box = fox)
- Recognize immediately (sight words)

Basic elements of phonics are consonants and vowels.

Teaching Phonics:
There are two main methods for teaching phonics: analytic and synthetic. With the analytic approach, consonants are generally not taught as individual pieces but are taught within a word.
  Example: *Dog* – /d/ is simply the sound at the beginning of the word. With the synthetic approach, words are decoded sound by sound.

Phonics
Knowledge of structural analysis as a word identification strategy

Orthography:
Orthography is the way of using a prescribed system to create words with letters that have meaning or spelling patterns.

Word Identification Strategies:
Structural Analysis (a.k.a. Morphology) – dividing words into syllables or meaningful parts. This is a seemingly simple task that many students struggle with. This strategy is usually introduced towards the end of the first grade and reinforced from the second grade onwards.

Structural Analysis – a word analysis strategy where a reader determines the meaning of an unfamiliar word by identifying prefixes, suffixes, and roots. This is very helpful in the Science and Language Arts classroom.

Prefix – an affix which is placed before the stem.
    Examples: un-, pre-, re-

Suffix – an affix which is placed after the stem. There are two kinds: inflectional and derivational.
- Inflectional – changes the grammatical properties, like changing the tense of the word.
  Examples: *-ed* past tense of the word, *-ing* progressive, *-n't* negative
- Derivational – changes parts of speech.
  Examples: adjective to adverb: -fy, -ly, -ful, -able, -ness, -less, -ism, -ment, -ist

Root/Stem – the part of the word that is common or the part that does not change.

Onset and Rime:
Words are formed from clusters of letters which represent sounds.
  Onset – is a consonant or cluster of consonants that comes at the beginning of a word; it comes before the vowels. If a word begins with a vowel, it has no onset.
  Rime – is the pattern of vowels and the consonants they are grouped with. In the word cook, 'c' is the onset and 'ook' is the rime.

Phonics
Spelling patterns and syllabication as techniques for decoding new words

Syllabication:
Syllabication is usually introduced in the second half of first grade and is formally taught in the second grade. This is roughly described as the division of words into syllables. Isn't this simple? Wrong. Many students struggle with this.

Teaching Syllabication – The two most commonly used methods are **generalizations** and **patterns**.
With the **generalization** method students are taught a series of rules.
- Affixes are usually one syllable.
- Compound words are at least two syllables.
- If there are two consonants between two vowels, the word usually divides in between the consonants.
- Words divide after single consonant after two vowels.
- Words divide between two vowels together.

With the **pattern** method, students examine a number of words that contain a high frequency syllable segment. (Advantage: students learn to pronounce recognizable units of multi-syllables).

Spelling Patterns:
Teachers often group 10 to 20 spelling words together that have a similar spelling. Doing this allows students to mentally group words together and notice patterns. This can be used when a student doesn't know how to spell a word. Here they can use one they do know from the list.

Phonics
Promoting decoding skills and word identification strategies

Decoding – describes the process a student goes through to break down and read words. Common methods used in the classroom to teach students to decode words are sounding out, analogous pairs, chunking, and context clues.
- Sounding Out – pronouncing the word letter by letter.
- Analogous Pairs – are similar words. For example, a student knows a word like "catch," so they may be able to decipher a word like "hatch." Catch and hatch are analogous pairs.
- Chunking – a process where the student groups letters into pronounceable sounds. Usually smaller than syllables, such as "at," this is found in words like h-at, c-at, and b-at.
- Context Clues – Students use their knowledge of the content to decode the words.

Encoding – can be described in reading as blending sounds and letters together to make new words. An example of this is sounding out a word in your mind and tying to write or spell it properly.

Phonics

Questions to Recap:

1. What is the first stage of reading?

2. Which is NOT a method of reading?
    a. By analogy
    b. Sound out
    c. Recognize immediately
    d. All of the above ARE methods of reading

3. Explain the difference between a prefix and a suffix.

4. _____ and _____ are two commonly used methods of teaching syllabication.

5. True or False: Encoding is a process used to break down and read words.

1.) pre-alphabetic stage 2.) d 3.) prefix comes before the stem, suffix comes after the stem 4.) generalization, patterns 5.) false

Vocabulary
Increasing students' vocabulary knowledge

The English language is a little complex with words that look alike, sound alike, or mean the same thing, or that look alike but mean something completely different. Knowing and understanding these things will increase students' overall vocabulary.

- **Synonym** – is a different word with a very similar meaning as the original, such as "happy" and "joyful." Students are encouraged to use the thesaurus to find alternate words.
- **Antonym** – is a word with an opposite meaning from the original, such as "inflate" and "deflate."
- **Homophone** – is a word that is pronounced the same as another but has a different meaning. These words may or may not be spelled the same, such as "to" and "two", "site" and "sight", "right" and "write."
- **Idiom** – is an expression, word, or phrase that has figurative or cultural meaning, that does not match the dictionary definition, like the phrase "*give up*."
- **Classification** – is a strategy that is important for students to know. This aids in comprehension and classifying words as similar or different.

Vocabulary

Strategies for improving vocabulary knowledge

Graphic Organizers:
These are tools that use visuals to organize information. These representations are used to clarify information. Examples are semantic maps, pictorial maps, and Venn Diagrams.

Semantic Map – a kind of graphic organizer that helps organize information into categories using blocks and lines. These help students build vocabulary and classification skills.

Steps to Complete:
1.) Introduce a word such as *pets* and ask students to suggest words that come to mind.
2.) List words on the board and make suggestions to help lead students to other words.
3.) Next, group words.
4.) Follow up by discussing the words used and reading about birds.

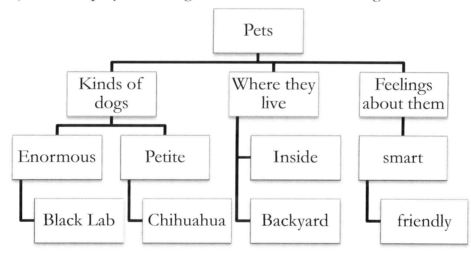

Pictorial Map – a type of graphic organizer that uses pictures and words to organize information. These can be used to differentiate instruction for visual learners.

Venn Diagrams – show relationship between two things, highlighting the similarities and differences.

Vocabulary
Strategies for improving vocabulary knowledge

Semantic Feature Analysis – a type of graphic organizer in grid form. Steps:
    1.) Introduce a topic, such as "sports"
    2.) List types of sports
    3.) Ask for characteristics or features of sports
    4.) Make suggestions for 2 and 3 if needed; lead with questions
    5.) Complete grid
        a. "+" if it has the characteristic
        b. "-" if it does not have the characteristic
    6.) Discuss grid – how are sports alike and different, then extend grid

Sports	Indoors	Outdoors	Grass	Court	Ball
Football	-	+	+	-	+
Baseball	-	+	+	-	+
Soccer	-	+	+	-	+
Hockey	+	+	-	-	+
Basketball	+	+	-	+	+
Tennis	+	+	+	+	+
Golf	-	+	+	-	+

Dramatizing – acting out a scene or skit using vocabulary. This helps student's associate words with the meaning.

Exploring Word Histories – students study the origins of words or text. This helps students in three ways: they remember longer, memory devices provide contexts and clues, sparks interest in words. This can be a fun project and students can develop research skills.

Enjoy Words – introduce students to crosswords puzzles or riddles.

Word of the Day – have a place in your classroom to show a word of the day and incorporate the word into class as many times as possible.

Vocabulary

How context is used to determine the meaning of unfamiliar words

Context Clues:
These are very helpful when students are learning to read at a more complex level. To utilize this concept, students are taught to find meaning within the text and to help formulate meaning for an unfamiliar word. Once students establish meaning, they use that information to aid in deciphering information.

When context does not work to decode vocabulary, or is not provided, there are other options for students:
- Pre-dictionaries – have pictures and contain fewer words.
- Glossaries – are found at the end of a text. They are helpful because there are fewer words and definitions and the words relate to the text.
- Dictionaries – using these improve skills like using alphabetical order and understanding meaning. Also, because some words have multiple meanings listed, students can decide which definition is appropriate using context clues.

It has been proven that students who utilize context clues are able to decipher seven times the number of words others decipher.

Vocabulary

Dictionaries and thesauruses for various purposes

To help build vocabulary it is important to have students utilize reference materials. Teachers can make a game out of this by encouraging students to use the new vocabulary. For example, have students use weekly vocabulary words in a sentence when asking to do something or go somewhere.

Vocabulary

Questions to Recap:

1. "Two" and "to" are known as _____.

2. Introducing a word and asking for suggestions of words that come to mind is the first step in creating a _____ map.

3. If a student cannot use context to identify a word meaning, which of these options is NOT an alternate method?
    a. Glossaries
    b. Idiom
    c. Dictionaries
    d. Pre-dictionaries

Fluency and Comprehension

Knowledge of rate, accuracy, expression, and phrasing in reading fluency

Fluency – The rate at which one reads without oral errors. The student must be able to pronounce or sound out the words; however, the student may or may not understand the word's meaning. Fluency is evaluated during oral reading.

The main components of fluency are accuracy, automaticity, rate, prosody.
- Accuracy – is the ability to pronounce or sound out a word and also to know the meaning.
- Automaticity – is a task that can be performed without attention or conscious effort.
- Rate – is how many words a student can read per minute; this increases with experience.
- Prosody – is a component of language that has to do with the rhythm of speech: pitch and stress. This is the expression, phrasing, or smoothness of a word, that is used to convey meaning.
    - Expression – how the students reads; i.e., with tone that matches the passage.
    - Phrasing – when words are read in chunks rather than word by word.
    - Smoothness – is like flow: how well does the student move from word to word, and is there hesitation in between each word.

To Improve Fluency:
- Choral reading – When students read aloud as a group, it helps them practice words.
- Model reading – This is done by the teacher and should be smooth and expressive; students should follow along.
- Rereading – This works because students improve speed and word recognition.
- One of the best ways to improve fluency is to read often and to read a variety of texts.

Fluency and Comprehension
Relationship between reading fluency and comprehension

Fluency and comprehension are often and easily confused. It is important to have a good understanding of each of these. Comprehension is an element within fluency and is reflected in the expression during oral reading or understanding during silent reading.

Comprehension – is being able to interpret the meaning of something written or spoken. This skill is crucial for literacy development.

A reader who is struggling with fluency will most likely struggle to get through a single sentence. When the student is bogged down with the mechanics of the words, the overall meaning of the sentence or paragraph is lost.

Fluency and Comprehension
Factors influencing reading comprehension

Many factors aid comprehension. Some of these include prior knowledge, context, vocabulary knowledge, and graphic cues.

Prior Knowledge – From birth we gain knowledge through experiences. Our brains store this information for later use. As students read about a post office, they draw on memories of their own trip to the post office.

Context – This is information found within the reading. This information is important for decoding unfamiliar words and aids in overall comprehension.

Vocabulary Knowledge – Students learn hundreds of new words every school year. Vocabulary knowledge is essential for comprehension. Many teachers enforce this by having students look up key vocabulary words before they start a new story. This ensures that students have been introduced to the new and unfamiliar words before they encounter them within the reading. This strategy is used in many subjects and grade levels.

Graphic Cues – are phrases or wording within readings that invoke a mental image. These cues describe things such as setting and time. For example, when a student reads "The moon kissed the horizon," The student will infer that it is night time, and envision the moon on the horizon.

Fluency and Comprehension
Literal, inferential, and evaluative comprehension

Literal Comprehension – is the most basic type of comprehension. This is what the passage/author clearly states. For example, look at the sentence "The rat sat on the mat." To check literal comprehension the teacher asks, "What sat on the mat?" or "What did the rat sit on?"

Inferential Comprehension – is the next level of comprehension. With this type of comprehension, students can draw conclusions and make predictions about outcomes. This type allows students to come up with the main idea and helps teachers to measure students' ability to interpret meaning from the passage. Students can answer questions that ask: who, what, when, where, why, and how.

Evaluative Comprehension – is probably the most difficult form of comprehension. With this type of comprehension the reader can offer an opinion based on the text. To do this the reader must understand fact and opinion. The student will be able to answer questions, such as "Why did you enjoy the story?" and "Do you think the story was well written?"

Fluency and Comprehension
Promoting students' literal, inferential, and evaluative comprehension

Literal Comprehension – This form of comprehension can be improved by having students follow along with their finger so that they can pick out the details within the reading. Also, having students reread a passage not only helps with fluency but aids literal comprehension.

Inferential Comprehension – To improve this type of comprehension, teachers can ask questions throughout the reading.

Evaluative Comprehension – This is a little more complex. To improve in this area, students must be taught how to form and pose questions. To practice this, students can write questions to ask the author.

Fluency and Comprehension

Strategies that aid comprehension before, during, and after reading

Factors/Strategies to Teach that Aid Comprehension:

Context – teaches students to use information within the story to aid understanding. This is also known as using context clues. (Also on page 32)

Prior Knowledge – what we already know about a topic. (Also on page 32)
    Example: – Snakes are reptiles.

Vocabulary Knowledge – When students already know and understand the vocabulary within the text, the teacher can facilitate this by introducing vocabulary before students read a story. (Also on page 32)

Graphic Cues – Using the clues from reading to visualize, such as when a student reads "The moon is full," the student imagines the size of the moon. This can be facilitated by having students read a passage and then draw a picture of what they saw in their "mind's eye." (Also on page 32)

Pre-Reading – Students can read about Anne Frank before reading about WWII. This will help students visualize and understand what it was like for the Jewish people in Germany during WWII.

Predicting – Having students read the title and ask them to make predictions about what the story is going to be about. It is also helpful to write these things down on the board so that students can discuss the predictions once reading is complete. This can be used across the curriculum.

Reread – After students finish reading the story the class can discuss the story and read it again.

Retelling – Ask students to read the story aloud or silently. Then, ask them to cover the story and tell the story to their neighbors. This helps students develop summarizing skills as well.

Relating Story to Real Life – This helps when students can make a personal connection. Students can tell their own story. Journal writing can be used here as well.

Fluency and Comprehension

Strategies that aid comprehension before, during, and after reading

Developing Literary Response Skills – This is a good way to ensure and detect comprehension. Have students write dialogues between themselves and the characters in a story they read.

** This information or writing could be written in "dialogue journals." These journals help teachers keep close contact with students and evaluate their comprehension.

Summarizing – is also an excellent strategy. It helps students understand the structure of text. It is also a great way to evaluate students' comprehension of a passage.

** Note: This takes a lifetime to master.

Questions to Recap:

1. A component of language that has to do with the rhythm of speech is called:
    a. Prosody
    b. Rate
    c. Automaticity
    d. Accuracy

2. What are the three types of reading comprehension?

3. What is one way to improve student's literal comprehension?

4. _____ is one of the factors that has an influence on reading comprehension.

1.) a   2.) literal, inferential, evaluative   3.) following along and rereading   4.) prior knowledge, context, vocabulary knowledge, graphic cues

Informational Texts and Literature
Types and characteristics of literature and informational texts

Informational Text:
There are four described qualities of informational text: accuracy, organization, design, and style. Within the text, the information should be current and complete. These texts are well researched and stereotypes should be avoided. The texts are also known as "Expository Texts."

Examples: ABCs and 123s, poetry and song, and multi-genre books that present information such as autobiographies, textbooks, and non-fiction.

Literary Text:
These are fictional and tell a story through prose, poetry, plays, etc.

Informational Texts and Literature
Literary elements and devices

Literary Elements:
Plot – The summary of events; what happened; a problem and how it is solved.

Four classic plots:
1.) Conflict between character and nature
2.) Conflict between character and society
3.) Conflict between characters
4.) Conflict within character

Characters – People or personified animals who are involved in the story.
Setting – Location of an event or story and time of day.
Point of View – Who is telling the story?
- First Person – through the eyes of character 'I.'
- Omniscient – author is god-like: sees and knows all.
- Limited Omniscient – Readers can know the thoughts of a character; also known as third person.
- Objective Viewpoint – Readers are eyewitnesses to the story but are confined to the immediate scene.

Theme – The underlying meaning of a story, it usually embodies general truths about human nature.

Informational Texts and Literature
Literary elements and devices

Literary Devices:
  Comparison – Authors compare one thing to another.
    Example: uses words such as *like* or *as*.
  Hyperbole – is when authors overstate or stretch the truth.
    Examples: It's raining cats and dogs.
  Imagery – Authors use descriptive or sensory words and phrases to create imagery or a picture in the reader's mind.
    Examples – The aroma of a turkey roasting in the oven filled grandmother's kitchen on Thanksgiving Day.
  Personification – gives human characteristics to animals or objects.
    Example – The moss crept over the sidewalk.
  Symbolism – uses a person, place, or thing to represent something else.
    Example – dove=peace, statue of liberty=freedom.
  Tone – overall feeling or effect in the story.
    Example – Cinderella makes you feel good.

Informational Texts and Literature
Literary response skills and making connections

It is important to relate text to students' personal experiences. This makes students more aware of the content because they can relate. Often teachers can use a literary text to introduce a new topic. The following are examples of making connections across the curriculum using reading and real life connections.

Examples of Making Connections:
- *'The Little Red Hen'* – During reading, students read the story of the little red hen, how the hen collects the wheat, processes the wheat, and how no one wants to help but then, once it is time to eat the bread, how everyone wants some. Ask students if they have ever done all of the work and someone wanted to take credit for the task.
- *'Diary of Anne Frank'* – During Social Studies, students are learning about WWII and they read an excerpt from "The Diary of Anne Frank." Then the teacher asks the students to imagine a time when they were sent to their rooms, only imagine being in their rooms for weeks.
- *'Picture 100 yards'* – During Math, students are learning about length. Sometimes it is hard to picture measurements, so the teacher can find something that is familiar to students. For yards, the teacher can have students picture a football field.
- *'Thickness of Earth's Crust'* – Can compare it to a driving distance students are familiar with.

Informational Texts and Literature

Knowledge of genres, themes, authors, and works of literature

There are six main types, or genres, in literature. They are: realistic, fiction, fantasy, folklore, poetry, and nonfiction.

Realistic Fiction – is a work of literature that is written with a realistic setting and with characters that face real-world problems. These real-world possibilities are within the range of what is possible in real life.

Characteristics:
- Real-world settings
- Themes dealing with human nature
- Natural spoken language
- Event that could happen (portrait of life)
- Characters that are representative of all types of people

Types:
- Contemporary Stories – stories that portray the real world and contemporary society
- Historical Fiction – realistic stories set in the past

Examples:
- *Because of Winn-Dixie,* by Kate DiCamillo
- *Harriet the Spy,* by Louise Fitzhugh
- *Anne of Green Gables,* by Lucy Maud Montgomery

Fantasy – is a work of literature with circumstances that could not occur in the natural scientific world. This genre is described as imaginative, supernatural, and magical; in this genre, anything is possible.

Types:
- Modern Literary Tales – Exemplify the characteristics of folk tales
- Fantastic Stories – Explore alternate realities and contain one or more elements not occurring naturally
- Science Fiction – Stories that explore scientific possibilities
- High Fantasy – Conflict between good and evil; involves quests

Examples:
- *Alice in Wonderland,* by Lewis Carroll
- Harry Potter Series, by J.K. Rowling
- *Matilda,* by Roald Dahl

Informational Texts and Literature
Knowledge of genres, themes, authors, and works of literature

Folklore or Folktales – are stories passed down by word of mouth, usually among people from the same region, culture, or country, through many generations.

Types:
- Fables – brief tales about morals
- Folk and Fairy Tales – triumph (good versus evil)
- Myths – usually created by ancient people to explain a natural phenomena
- Legends – tall tales of courage and good deeds

Examples:
- John Henry – famous for challenging a steam-powered hammer and winning, only to die immediately after with his hammer in his hand.
- Paul Bunyan – mythological lumberjack, a very large man with exceptional strength, he is often paired with a large blue ox in stories.

Poetry – is an individual piece of writing with rhythms, rhymes, and flow. They sometimes follow strict rules or can be free form.

Types:
- Formula Poems – Like recipes, these are not rigid. Examples include the "I wish…" poem, color poem, and the five senses poem.
- Free-Form Poem – Students choose words that describe something and put them together without worrying about arrangement or rhyme. Example: Concrete poems have words arranged to form a picture.
- Syllable and Word Count Poems – provide students with structure for writing. Examples: Haiku – a Japanese poem that is 17 syllables arranged in 3 lines of 5-7-5.
- Rhymed Verse Forms – adhere to strict rhyming pattern/scheme. Example: Limerick – a five-line poem where lines 1, 2, and 5 rhyme and lines 3 and 4 rhyme with each other and are shorter.
- Model Poems – Students model their poems after other poems.

Informational Texts and Literature
Knowledge of genres, themes, authors, and works of literature

Nonfiction – are works written to inform a reader about a subject. The information within is considered to be fact.

Types:
- Informational – contain ideas, facts, and principles that are true or factual.
  Examples: articles of fact, essays of fact, manuals, picture books, and textbooks.
- Reference – compilations of information.
  Examples: dictionary, encyclopedia, atlas, and almanac.
- Biography – A true story about a person's life.
- Autobiography – A true story about a person's life written by that person.

Themes – are the messages within the story. The theme encompasses general truths about human nature. Themes can be spelled out or implied.
- Authors – compose works of fiction and non-fiction.
- Works of literature for children – there are literally thousands of children's books. There are different types, such as picture books, short stories, and chapter books, but they have one central feature – something is learned or enforced, whether it is a moral, a lesson, or a value.

Informational Texts and Literature

Organizational patterns in informational texts

Expository (Informational) Text Structures:

Description – The author describes a topic by listing characteristics, features, and examples.
    Possible Cue Words: for example

Sequence – The author lists items in chronological order.
    Possible Cue Words: first, second, next, then, finally

Comparison – The author explains how two or more things are alike or different.
    Possible Cue Words: like, same as

Cause and Effect – The author lists causes and then the resulting effect(s).
    Possible Cue Words: if…then, because, therefore

Problem and Solution – The author states a problem and lists solutions for the problem.
    Possible Cue Words: problem is, solved, question

Informational Texts and Literature

Promoting comprehension of informational texts

Main Idea – is the implied meaning of the passage; also called a summary statement. The main idea is usually determined using explicit and implicit details.
- Explicit details – specific details; these are easy to pick out.
- Implicit details – implied details or meaning; these are not as easy to pick out.

Glossary – These are little dictionaries found within content area text. These are easy to use and contain only words and phrases used in the text.

Graphic Organizer – devices used to organize information

Story Map:

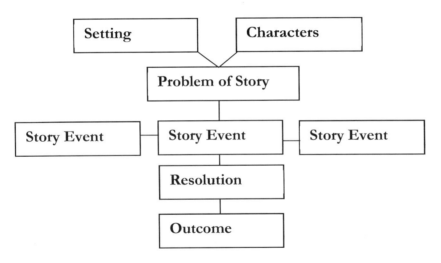

KWL's:

What I **K**now	**W**ant to Know	What I **L**earned

Informational Texts and Literature
Promoting comprehension of informational texts

How to Teach Students to Find the Main Idea:
- First, students need to learn to classify things. To get students started, bring in several objects and have students classify them into categories. Then work as a group to give each category a title. Once students understand classifying objects, then show students a list of words which include a category title within.
  Examples: cats, fish, dogs – pets
  Examples: apple, peach, maple – trees

- Second, students learn to recognize topic sentences. Explain that the main idea of a paragraph is also known as the topic sentence because it contains the topic of the paragraph.

This takes time and needs lots of practice. Repeat practice with the use of modeling and using examples as far as possible.

Questions to Recap:

1. The main idea of a passage is also called a _____ statement.

2. Name three literary elements of a story.

3. Name three literary devices.

4. Informational, reference, biography, and autobiography are all types of_____ literature.

1.) summary   2.) plot, characters, setting, point of view, theme   3.) comparison, hyperbole, imagery, personification, symbolism, tone   4.) nonfiction

Writing
Developmental stages of spelling and handwriting

Developmental Spelling – Stages of Spelling:
- Scribble – around 18 months old
- Word-like scribble – around 3 years old
- Prephonemic writing – around 4-5 years old
- Alphabetic writing – around 4-7 years old
- Word within word writing – around 6-7 years old
- Syllable connections – 8+ years old

Handwriting – Stages of Handwriting:
Basic handwriting skills in kindergarten
- How to hold pencil
- Writing upper and lower case letters

Transition to cursive handwriting
- Students are introduced to cursive handwriting in grades two or three. They learn to read and write cursive letters.

Writing

Factors in writing for audiences, purposes, genres, formats, and modes

Audience – Students should be aware that all writing is for someone, even if they plan to have no one read what they have written. Explain that they will be reading what they write.

Writing for an audience: questions students can ask themselves
- Who am I writing for?
- What is my topic?
- What do I want my audience to know?

Purpose – Students need to decide why they are writing; also to decide if they want to entertain, inform, or persuade.

Writing Genres – formats for writing
- Descriptive writing – observations, descriptive sentences
- Informal writing – autobiographies, biographies, dictionaries, and reports
- Journals and letters – emails, business letters
- Persuasive writing – advertisements, movie reviews
- Poetry – color poems, Haiku's, 'I am' poems
- Story writing

Modes of Writing, or Types of Writing – As a student in English 101 or 1101, you likely practiced most of these types: descriptive, persuasive, evaluative, narrative, compare and contrast, and cause and effect.

Writing
The writing process

Prewriting – To write, students need to have a plan. During this stage, students choose a topic, consider purpose, form, and audience. Students also come up with ideas and organize ideas for writing.

Drafting – To perfect writing, students write and rewrite their composition. During the first draft, students should concentrate on simply getting their thought onto paper.

Revising – This stage is all about refining ideas to ensure that the paper has meaning and purpose.

Steps for revising:
- Read the rough draft
- Peer review
- Revise based on feedback
- Conference with the teacher

Editing – In this stage, the student's writing is put into final form for proofreading and correcting.

Publishing – Students bring their compositions to life and share them with classmates and/or parents through books or reading from the author's chair.

Writing
Using writing strategies and language to achieve various effects

Point of View:
- First Person Viewpoint – is told through the eyes of a character within the story; uses "I."
- Omniscient Viewpoint – The author knows and sees all
- Limited Omniscient Viewpoint – This is used so that the reader can know the thoughts of one character; this is known as third person point of view.
- Objective Viewpoint – Readers are eye witnesses to the story and are confined to the immediate scene.

Author's Voice – The author sets the tone for the story: happy, sad, or inspirational.

Establishing Setting – This is an integral part of writing. Descriptions of the setting invoke mental images of sand, night, cold, and wind.

Sensory Details – These are descriptions of senses and emotion, such as describing the smell of popcorn and the sounds and aroma of a fair or carnival.

Writing
Ways to improve the written materials

The process of revising should be practiced and, therefore, modeled for the students. To practice, students can trade papers and critique each other's writing. Also, the students can be given samples that need editing.

During this time, students can also be placed into "writing groups."
1.) Students take turns reading each other's compositions aloud.
2.) Students say what they liked or enjoyed about the composition.
3.) After the positive comments writers ask for assistance with trouble areas.
4.) The group makes suggestions to improve the writing.
5.) The first four steps are repeated for each student.
6.) The writers make choices of what revisions to make.

After this process is repeated a few times students become each other's advocates.

Writing
Research skills and computer technology to support writing

Report Writing: is slightly different from story writing. This can seem overwhelming to students, so it is important to go through the steps slowly, taking days to model and practice each step.

- **Students Need to Know the Nature and Purpose of the Assignment** – Relate this to life; for example, when will they use this again. Explain that this is how their textbooks were written.
- **Choosing a Topic** – Guide students and give them lists to choose from.
- **Collect Materials** – Teach them how to use the library (demonstrate and model this). This is also when you can teach students how to find valid internet resources because the amount of information found online can be overwhelming. Limit the number of sites the students can visit.
- **Direct Instruction on How to Identify Information** – It is important to model this.
- **Note Taking** – Some students have no idea how to take notes. While reading the information, this needs to be practiced.
- **Compile and Organize Information.**

Then follow the writing process. **(From page 46)**

Writing

Questions to Recap:

1. Which is not a point of view in a literary work?
    a. Omniscient viewpoint
    b. Sensory viewpoint
    c. First person viewpoint
    d. Objective viewpoint

2. How old are students when they start to make syllable connections?

3. Name three of the steps in the writing process.

1.) b 2.) 8+ 3.) prewriting, drafting, revising, editing, publishing

English Grammar
Parts of speech

Noun – A word that is used to name something – a person, a place, or a thing. There are two types of nouns – proper and common.
- Proper noun – The name of a person, place, or thing; always capitalized.
  Examples: Matthew, Dean, Jennifer, Georgia
- Common noun – is not particular and not capitalized.
  Example: dog, sandwich

Pronoun – A word used in the place of a noun.
Examples: I, you, it, me, who, we, they, us

Adjective – A word that describes a noun or pronoun.
Example: melted, white, magical

Verb – A word that shows action, or a state of being.
Example: walk, jog, run, skip, stand, be

Adverb – A word used to modify a verb, an adjective, or another adverb. An adverb answers the questions where, why, how often, and how much.
Examples: inside, faster, noisily, quickly

Preposition – A word or group of words used to show position or direction, or how two words or ideas are related to each other.
Examples: above, at, before, down, in, in front of, inside of, like, near

Conjunction – A word that connects words.
Examples: and, but, or, either, because, when

Interjection – A word or phrase used to express strong emotion, set off by commas or an exclamation point.
Examples: Wow!, Cool, Oh!

English Grammar
Knowledge of grammar and usage

Subject-Verb Agreement – Does your subject/noun agree with your verb?
- Two or more nouns need a plural verb – are
- One noun needs a singular verb – is
  Example: Many people is/<u>are</u> waiting outside.
  Example: The print of the labels <u>is</u>/are so small.

Noun-Pronoun Agreement – ensure that number and gender match

Noun	Pronoun	Wrong
John	He	Not they or she
Ben and Jerry	They	Not he or she
Dog	It	Not they

Verb Tense – past, present and future
   Examples: walked, walk, will walk

English Grammar
Mechanics of writing

Spelling – This is an important writing convention and should be correct at all times. Students may use traditional spelling rules like phonics, memorization, or dictionaries to have the correct spelling for the words.

Punctuation – This covers a broad field; however, the most common are commas and sentence endings. Commas are used to separate items within a series, between two or more adjectives, before coordinating conjunctions in a compound sentence, to separate the date from year, between city and state, and to separate a quotation from the rest of the sentence. See sentence structure for sentence endings, page 53.

English Grammar
Mechanics of writing

Capitalization:

- All proper nouns must be capitalized, as well as the pronoun "I."
- Capitalize words used as names or parts of names – Aunt Sue.
- First word in the sentence must be capitalized.
- Capitalize important words in titles of publications – essays, books, journals, and stories.
- Capitalize specific course titles – English 1100.
- Capitalize the names of months and the days of the week.
- Capitalize the first letter of names of people, organizations, and places.
- Titles must be capitalized when they precede a name – Mr., Sir, Dr. and Miss.
- Capitalize adjectives that are made from the names of people and places. Example: I enjoy **S**outhern food.
- Capitalize initials and acronyms. (Acronyms are words formed by the first or first few letters of words in the name of an organization.)
- Capitalize directions only when they are used to designate actual geographic locations, not when they point in a direction. Examples: the **S**outh, the **M**idwest, but not head **e**ast.
- Capitalize historical events, documents, and time periods. Examples: the Great Depression, Gettysburg Address.
- Capitalize the name of languages, races, nationalities, cultures, and religions. Examples: **E**nglish, **N**ative **A**mericans, **I**rish, **C**ajun, and **C**atholic.

English Grammar
Correcting errors in sentence structure

Run-on Sentences – lack necessary punctuation, such as commas and semicolons.
- I have got to run my sister says it's time to go. (Run-on)
- I have got to run. My sister says it's time to go. (Correct)

Misplaced Modifiers – are words or phrases that may cause confusion because they are not close enough in meaning to the word they are modifying.
- My cat was hit by a car running across the road. (Was the car or the cat running across the road?)

Sentence Fragments – are incomplete sentences.
- A story with deep thought and emotion.

English Grammar
Types of sentence structures

Sentence Structures:
Sentences are made of dependent and independent clauses.
- Independent clause – A part of a sentence that can stand alone because it makes sense by itself. Each independent clause contains a subject and a verb.
- Dependent clause – A group of words that has a subject and a verb. It cannot stand alone and does not make sense by itself in a sentence. A dependent clause has to be attached to an independent clause in order to make sense.

Types of Sentence Endings:
  Declarative – Makes a statement.
    Example: The dogs are sleeping on the couch. Punctuation: ".", a period
  Interrogative – Asks a question.
    Example: Did you forget your keys again? Punctuation: "?", a question mark
  Imperative – Makes a command.
    Example: Turn on the light. Punctuation: ".", a period
  Exclamation – Shows strong emotion or surprise
    Example: Oh my goodness! Punctuation: "!", an exclamation mark

English Grammar
Types of sentence structures

Main Types of Sentences:
There are four main types of sentences: simple, compound, complex, and compound-complex.

    Simple – A sentence that is made of a single independent clause.
        Example: The cat ran.
    Compound – A sentence that is made of two independent clauses.
        Example: The cat ran, but the cat did not leave the room.
    Complex – A sentence that is made of one independent clause and one or more dependent clauses.
        Example: When the cat ran, he was not afraid.
    Compound-Complex – A sentence that is made of two independent clauses and one or more dependent clauses.
        Example: When the cat ran, he did not leave the room like I thought.

English Grammar

Questions to Recap:

1. The first part of the test was over biology, the second <u>over mathematics, and the third over english.</u>

    a. over mathematics, and the third over english.
    b. over mathematics; and the third over English.
    c. over Mathematics; and the third over English.
    d. over mathematics, and the third over English.

2. As a result of his method for early music education, Ken Clinton <u>has been known as one</u> of America's great synchronized swimmers.

    a. is seen as one
    b. is being seen as one
    c. has been known as one
    d. had been known as one

3. After having his tonsels removed, the child was listless for a few days.

    a. Capitalization
    b. Punctuation
    c. Spelling
    d. Grammar

1.) d 2.) a 3.) c

Reading and Writing across the Curriculum
Verbal interactions of one-on-one and groups

It is important to foster verbal interactions with students. Students should be familiar with taking turns and responding to questions with the correct information. The best ways to improve these things are through practice and modeling. Also, to ensure fairness, teachers should incorporate some kind of equity system for calling on students. Some ideas are using playing cards or Popsicle sticks with students' names.

Reading and Writing across the Curriculum
Strategies for promoting listening

Students can participate in note taking activities, making outlines as the speaker talks. Students can quiz each other.
The teacher can read a passage out loud and ask questions about the passage. This helps with comprehension. The students can teacher each other in small groups (Jigsaw).

Reading and Writing across the Curriculum
Verbal cues and body language as communication

Envision a woman standing with her arms crossed and a frown. She doesn't have to say a word but you know right away that she is mad. Body language is a very effective form of communication and highly effective in the classroom. Simply making eye contact with a student allows them to know you see them and what they are doing. Your voice is also another powerful weapon; it can be filled with expressions of sympathy, displeasure, and praise.

Reading and Writing across the Curriculum
Recognizing types, characteristics, and roles of visual and oral media

Students can view and listen to a multitude of media. Students can learn about new topics, identify the point of view, persuasive technique used, and arguments in an advertisement or within a story through the use of visual media. Visual media includes photos, slides, film strips, video clips, and entire videos.

Reading and Writing across the Curriculum
Knowledge of the structures and elements of presentations

Presentations are becoming a daily part of everyday lessons, but it is important to ensure that all learning modalities are addressed within the presentation.

Hands on activities can be incorporated throughout the presentations. Also students can be broken up into pairs or small groups.

Questions to Recap:

1. Name two strategies for promoting listening among students.

2. Using your voice to show praise is an example of _____.

3. Visual media include:
    a. Photos
    b. Books
    c. Movies
    d. All of the above

1.) note taking, outlines, jigsaw 2.) verbal cues 3.) d

Social Studies:

This section is organized according to the frameworks available in PDF format from the GACE website www.gace.nesinc.com. There are four objectives for this section.

Items in this section:
- ☑ History
- ☑ Geography
- ☑ Government
- ☑ Economics

***Note: Some information may be repeated between the history and government sections.

Georgia, U.S., and World History Events

Recognizing that historical events are related and influence diverse people

It is important for students to understand that historical events follow a chronological time line. It is also important for students to understand that history is a cause and effect relationship. Below you will find PEOPLE IN HISTORY from "Georgia Standards for Grades K-5," people who are significant to historical events.

Benjamin Franklin – Inventor, author, and statesman; flew a kite in a thunderstorm to prove the conduction of electricity.

Thomas Jefferson – Main author of the Declaration of Independence.

Lewis & Clark with Sacagawea – Explored from St. Louis to Pacific Coast, the lands of the Louisiana Purchase; took two years and four months.

Harriet Tubman – Underground Railroad; helped free over 300 slaves.

Theodore Roosevelt – The first president to consider National Parks and the Environment.

George Washington Carver – African scientist, botanist, and inventor.

Paul Revere – Well known for his involvement in independence; rode through the streets shouting, 'The British are coming,' in his well-known Midnight Ride.

Fredrick Douglas – African American involved in civil rights. He believed in equality, and he was a slave who escaped and learned to read.

Susan B. Anthony – A civil rights leader and prominent American who played a major role in the 19th Century Women's Right Movement.

Mary McLeod Bethune – African American woman, educator, and civil rights leader; she was best known for starting a school for black students.

Franklin D. Roosevelt – Well known for his involvement in the New Deal and WWII. The New Deal was a package of economic programs to promote relief, reform, and recovery.

Eleanor Roosevelt – First Lady to Franklin D. Roosevelt; worked for human rights, specifically among working women, and supported New Deal.

Thurgood Marshall – First African American on the United State Supreme Court; was present for the Brown vs. Board of Education Case.

Georgia, U.S., and World History Events

Recognizing that historical events are related and influence diverse people

Lyndon B. Johnson – Well known for his idea of 'The Great Society,' aka social reform, elimination of poverty and voting rights. LBJ was the 36th president; he completed Kennedy's term and was then elected president again.

Cesar Chavez – a Mexican American farm worker and civil rights activist.

Georgia, U.S., and World History Events

The importance of events and issues in Georgia, U.S., and world history

American Revolution:
  Events Leading to the American Revolution:
- French & Indian War, aka War of Conquest, aka Seven Years War – Parties involved also included French, English, and Americans. This was one of the bloodiest wars. It took place because everyone wanted their "piece" of the New World. During this time, Indians fought on both sides. The war ended with the Treaty of Paris.
- British Imperial Policy – This led to the 1765 Stamp Act, which was supposed to help pay for men stationed in North America. The famous slogan, "No taxation without representation," came from this.
- Activities of the Sons of Liberty – These American patriots were responsible for the Boston Tea Party, which was an act of direct defiance of the British. To protest the Tea Act, they dumped boxes of tea into the harbor.

Declaration of Independence:
The document was written primarily by Thomas Jefferson, though a committee of five was assembled to create the document. This committee consisted of John Adams, Benjamin Franklin, Thomas Jefferson, Robert R. Livingston, and Roger Sherman. The declaration consists of five sections, including charges against the King and reasons why America should be separated from Great Britain. This document was a response to the tyranny and abuse of power Britain held over America, and it gave the colonists a voice.

Georgia, U.S., and World History Events

The importance of events and issues in Georgia, U.S., and world history

Significant People in the American Revolution:
- King George III – King of Great Britain
- George Washington – First president and commander of the Continental Army in the American Revolution
- Benjamin Franklin – One of the founding fathers who aided in the Declaration of Independence
- Thomas Jefferson – Drafted the Declaration of Independence
- Benedict Arnold – General during the American Revolution who switched sides from the American to the British
- Patrick Henry – Famous for saying, "Give me liberty, or give me death"
- John Adams – second president of the U.S. and the first Vice President

Major Battles of the American Revolution:
- Lexington and Concord – first military battle of the war
- Saratoga – two battles took place here
- Yorktown – battle that led to the Treaty of Paris

New Government:
The United States modeled itself somewhat after Greece. You can see this when you see the Parthenon and the U.S. Supreme Court building. Athens has a direct democracy, and the U.S. adopted a representative democracy. Athenians choose their leaders as we do.
- Weaknesses of the Article of Confederation – came from the fear of placing too much power in the wrong hands.
- Leaders of the Constitutional Convention – James Madison and Benjamin Franklin; major issue they debated was the rights of the states.
- The Great Compromise – offered two houses of government with equal representation in the senate or upper house. The size of each state would be represented in the House based on population. (When population was introduced into this, the South wanted to count their slaves and the North did not.)
- Three Branches of Government – Executive-President, Legislative-Congress, and Judicial-Supreme Court.
- The Constitution – The Bill of Rights were introduced to it in 1791 by James Madison because he believed we all have certain rights. These are the first ten amendments to the Constitution.

Georgia, U.S., and World History Events

The importance of events and issues in Georgia, U.S., and world history

War of 1812:
  Causes of the War:
  - Great Britain's interference with America's trading with France and other nations.
  - Dispute over land in the northern territories.
  - Great Britain's search for deserters on American merchant ships.

  Effects of this War:
  - Led to the end of the Federalist Party.
  - Caused growth of American industries.
  - Confirmed the status of the United States as a free and independent nation.
  - The Capital and the White House were burned.

Expansion of America between 1801 and 1861:
  Louisiana Purchase – extended westward migration across the Appalachians; expanded American territory; this more than doubled the size of America.
  Lewis and Clark – were given the job to explore the new purchase from St. Louis to the Pacific Coast. It took them two years and four months.
  Acquisition of Texas (Alamo & Independence) – Texas was won from Mexico. Texas hoped to be independent but didn't get it; then joined the Union.
  Oregon (Oregon Trail) – This was the path people from the East Coast took to move to the Wild West. It started in Independence, Missouri, and ended in Portland, Oregon. Some people walked other rode in buggies.
  California (Gold Rush) – Gold fever had a massive impact on westward expansion, changing the population of California from 400 to 44,000 within two years.

  Major Inventions of this Time:
  - Steamboats – These steam powered boats went up and down the Mississippi and made moving goods more economical, and thus trade developed.
  - Steam Locomotive – transformed the Northeast into the center of American Commerce.
  - Telegraph – improved shipping and commerce in the United States.

Georgia, U.S., and World History Events

The importance of events and issues in Georgia, U.S., and world history

Impact of Expansion on the Native Americans – They were driven further and further west towards the Northwest, shrinking the size of the tribes.

The Civil War 1861-1865:
  Causes of the Civil War:
  - *Uncle Tom's Cabin* – Written by Harriet Beecher Stowe, this book let everyone glance into the life of a slave named Tom.
  - John Brown's raids on Harper's Ferry – John Brown, with both white and black men, tried to raid the federal arsenal, but they were killed.
  - Slavery – The South seceded from the Union. The North and South became more divided about slavery.

  Major Battles of the Civil War:
  - Fort Sumter – When Fort Sumter fell to the Confederates, it united the North, and when Lincoln called for volunteers, the response was overwhelming. This caused more states to secede from the Union.
  - Gettysburg – The Confederacy lost its steam during this battle. They lost 28,000 men and surrendered the next day in Vicksburg.
  - The Atlanta Campaign – included a number of battles fought throughout northwest Georgia and the area around Atlanta, which led to the eventual fall of Atlanta and brought the Civil War to an end faster.
  - Sherman's March to the Sea – Sherman and the Union Army marched through Atlanta, burning cities along the way. He wanted to make southern states so sick of war that they would not want to enter another war for years.
  - Appomattox Court House – was where Lee and Grant met to arrange the surrender of the South. This ended the four-year war.

Georgia, U.S., and World History Events

The importance of events and issues in Georgia, U.S., and world history

The Civil War 1861-1865 (cont'd)
Effects of the Civil War on the North and South:
- Reconstruction in the South (scalawags and carpetbaggers)
- Southern Poverty – Many southern people lost their homes and livelihood as a result of the war.
- Jim Crow laws – mandated separate but equal facilities be provided to African Americans.
- Slaves were freed.

Resulting Constitutional Amendments:
- 13th Amendment abolished slavery in the U.S.
- 14th Amendment included slaves as U.S. citizens.
- 15th Amendment stated that citizens cannot be denied the right to vote based on race or the color of their skin.

Freedmen's Bureau – A government agency that aided the refugees of the Civil War – mostly slaves – with education, health care, and employment.

Important People during the Civil War:
- Abraham Lincoln – 16th president, served during the Civil War. It was he who preserved the Union and ended slavery.
- Ulysses S. Grant – Chief General during the Civil War for the Union; later became President.
- Thomas "Stonewall" Jackson – Confederate general during the Civil War, present in many of the major battles and Bull Run.
- Robert E. Lee – General for the Confederates, he later surrendered at Appomattox.
- Jefferson Davis – served as president of the Confederates. After the war, he was charged with treason.

Georgia, U.S., and World History Events

The importance of events and issues in Georgia, U.S., and world history

Turn of the Century and Change in America:

Black Cowboys of Texas – Around 5,000 black men worked as cowboys and herded cattle.

Great Western Cattle Trail – This trail ran parallel to the Chisholm Trail. It was used to move herd east. It started in San Antonio, Texas, and ended in Dodge City, Kansas.

Chisholm Trail – connected Texas to Kansas.

Wright Brothers – are credited with inventing and flying the first successful airplane.

George Washington Carver – made strides in agricultural science; instrumental in the reconstruction of the south; introduced peanuts to the South.

Alexander Graham Bell – revolutionized phone communication.

Thomas Edison – invented many things but is most famous for the modern light bulb and the phonograph.

William McKinley – 25th president; last veteran of the American Civil War.

Theodore Roosevelt – 26th president, aka Teddy; his image is on Mount Rushmore.

Immigration to the U.S. Why?
- These people were looking for a better life. The influx of people was made easier because of newer boats and ships. Refugees from foreign countries sought refuge in America.
- From the late 1800s to the early 1900s, over 30 million people migrated to the U.S., many of whom came through Ellis Island.
- People left Europe and Russia because of religious persecution. Entire villages of Jews were driven from Russia. People left Europe because it was getting overcrowded and jobs were hard to find. America offered plentiful jobs, independence, and opportunity.
- People came from China and Japan by way of the West Coast. They came to find gold in California during the gold rush.
- People in Texas became citizens when it was annexed to the Union.

Georgia, U.S., and World History Events
The importance of events and issues in Georgia, U.S., and world history

Westward Expansion:
The main reasons for westward expansion were the search for silver and gold and homesteading.
Homestead Act – brought people west. It offered 160 acres of land for free to anyone who would live and cultivate it for five years.
Impact on Native Americans – They were pushed further and further away and displaced.
Battle of Little Bighorn and Relocation of Native Americans to Reservations – General Custer is known for this battle. Custer arrived with 1500 tired men and horses. They were met by 2000-3000 Native Americans warriors. Within twenty minutes, Custer and all of his men were dead.

Georgia, U.S., and World History Events
The importance of events and issues in Georgia, U.S., and world history

World War I (1914-1918):
  Causes for the War:
  - Imperialism – European rivalries arose as industry compctition grew. Great Britain, France, Germany, Austria-Hungary, Russia, and Italy wanted to expand their markets and global empire.
  - Nationalism – The belief that national interests should be placed ahead of global interests.
  - Militarism – As tensions rose, so did the glorification of war and the military.
  - Alliance System – Along with militarism came a hardening of alliances.
  - Sinking of the Lusitania – A German U-boat sank this ship. The Germans defended their actions because the boat was carrying ammunition and explosives. This solidified America's entry into the war.

  Sides:
  - Allied Powers – Russia, France, and Britain, as well as many other countries, including Canada, Greece, Italy, Japan, and Romania.
  - Central Powers – The alliance between Germany and Austria-Hungary. The Ottoman Empire joined later.

Georgia, U.S., and World History Events

The importance of events and issues in Georgia, U.S., and world history

World War I (1914-1918) (cont'd.):
Effects of the War:
- Nine million soldiers died and 21 million were wounded*
- Thirteen million civilians died from starvation and disease*
- The Treaty of Versailles in 1919 ended WWI. It had several weaknesses: it stripped Germany of its Air Force and limited its Army. This humiliation led Germany to an even greater violence in the form of Nazism.

Numbers may be different per source; use numbers as an indication of tragedy.

Key People of WWI:
- George Clemenceau (France)
- David Lloyd George (Britain)
- Vittorio Orlando (Italy)
- President Woodrow Wilson (U.S.)
- Archduke Franz Ferdinand, heir to Austria-Hungary throne.
- Emperor Nicholas II (Russia)
- Emperor Wilhelm II (Germany)
- Emperor Franz Josef (Austria-Hungary)

The Great Depression & the New Deal:
- Stock Market Crash of 1929 – Banks failed; stock markets collapsed; continued for a month. The roaring '20s led to the crash, and some people lost everything.
- Herbert Hoover – was a mining engineer and the 31st president, right after the crash and through the Great Depression.
- Franklin Roosevelt – 32nd president, created the New Deal and was reelected.
- Dust Bowl – result of severe drought, affected 100 million acres.
- Soup Kitchens – became mainstream during the Great Depression.
- New Deal – The unemployment rate was 25% or higher. This program was designed to alleviate the problems of the Great Depression, focusing on relief for the needy, economic recovery, and financial reform.

Georgia, U.S., and World History Events
The importance of events and issues in Georgia, U.S., and world history

The 1930s:
- Duke Ellington – influential figure in Jazz; toured in the U.S. and Europe.
- Margaret Mitchell – wrote *Gone with the Wind*; won a Pulitzer.
- Jesse Owens – First African American to win an Olympic Gold medal; won in track and field.

Georgia, U.S., and World History Events
The importance of events and issues in Georgia, U.S., and world history

World War II (1939 – 1945):
  Causes of the War:
- Japan was expanding into Asia.
- Italy wanted Ethiopia.
- Spanish Civil War.
- Hitler started expanding – Austria was first annexation; the Holocaust.

Allied Powers: Great Britain, France, United States, and the Soviet Union.
Axis Powers: Germany, Italy, and Japan.

Effects and Battles of the War:
- Pearl Harbor – marked U.S. entry into the war.
- Iwo Jima – Japanese island and battle site during WWII.
- D-Day – June 6, 1944; the day the Allies launched an invasion into Europe.
- VE-Day – when Eisenhower accepted the surrender of the Nazis.
- VJ-Day – victory over Japan; when they surrendered.
- Holocaust – 6 million Jews systematically killed by the Nazis.*
- 55 million dead in all.*
- Women entered the workforce.
- The decision to drop bombs on Hiroshima and Nagasaki. Truman decided it would be the best way to strike the Japanese hard and fast.
- United Nations was formed as an international peacekeeping organization to which most of the nations in the world belong; founded in 1945 to promote world peace, security, and economic development.

Numbers may be different per source; use numbers as an indication of tragedy.

Georgia, U.S., and World History Events

The importance of events and issues in Georgia, U.S., and world history

World War II (1939 – 1945): cont.
People of WWII:
- Roosevelt – president during WWII; wanted to Americanize everywhere.
- Stalin – became the leader of the Soviet Union; wanted to purge the communist party.
- Churchill – led the United Kingdom during WWII and received the Nobel Prize in Literature.
- Hirohito – emperor of Japan during WWII; ally with Germany.
- Truman – 33rd president; had many domestic challenges during a troubled economy.
- Mussolini – Italian politician; established a totalitarian regime in Italy. He wanted to change Italy's political outlook.

Effects of Rationing and the Changing Role of Women and African Americans:
- Rosie the Riveter – cultural icon of the U.S.; symbolized the woman in the workforce.
- Tuskegee Airmen – African American pilots who flew with distinction during WWII.

United Nations – An international peacekeeping organization to which most of the nations in the world belong; founded in 1945 to promote world peace, security, and economic development.

Georgia, U.S., and World History Events

The importance of events and issues in Georgia, U.S., and world history

Cold War and Civil Rights:
  Iron Curtain – symbolized the physical boundary dividing Europe into two separate areas, from the end of WWII to the end of the Cold War.
  Berlin Airlift – Created to bring supplies to Berlin, the Soviet Union blocked supplies being brought in any other way.

Korean War:
  Causes – South Korea was invaded by North Korea. When World War II ended, Japan annexed Korea. At the end of World War II, America and Great Britain created a democratic government in the southern part of Korea, and the Soviet Union set up a communist government in the northern part. The Korean War was an attempt to use force to unify all of Korea under Communist rule. After the invasion, the United States and United Nations came to South Korea's defense. This war still continues today.
  Effects – After China backed North Korea, both sides decided the peninsula should be divided into two hostile neighbors. As a result, American troops are stationed in South Korea to protect it against attacks from the north.

North Atlantic Treaty Organization – is the treaty that brought NATO into existence.
Joseph McCarthy – A politician who thought there were many spies in the U.S. He was eventually discredited.
Nikita Khrushchev – Soviet leader responsible for partial de-Stalinization of the Soviet Union; backed space program and liberal reform.
Cuban Missile Crisis – was when the Soviet Union placed missiles in Cuba.

Vietnam War:
  Causes – Like the Korean War in Vietnam, communism was spreading, and America decided it needed to slow its progress. This war was an attempt to slow the progression.
  Effects – This war was lost because as communism spread, Americans were overtaken. Americans fled Vietnam, and it became a communist county.

Georgia, U.S., and World History Events

The importance of events and issues in Georgia, U.S., and world history

Brown v. BOE – allowed blacks and whites to attend school together, through integration.
Montgomery Bus Boycott – protested the company's policy on racial segregation.
March on Washington – when Martin Luther King, Jr., marched for jobs and freedom and gave his "I have a dream" speech.
Civil Rights Act – was to ensure voting rights for African Americans.
Voting Rights Act – outlawed discriminatory voting practices.
Rosa Parks – African American civil rights activist, who refused to move to the back of the bus.

Key Assassinations:
- John F. Kennedy – 35th president, during Cold War.
- Robert F. Kennedy – assassinated while running for president.
- Martin Luther King, Jr. – shot in hotel room.

Georgia, U.S., and World History Events

Native American cultures in North America and interactions with early explorers

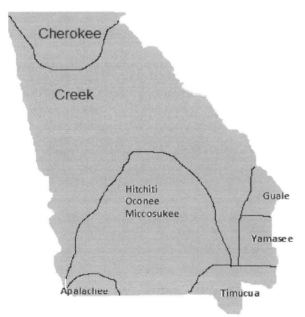

Georgia Indians:
Georgia Creek – were around before the Cherokee, and occupied most of Georgia. They slowly lost power and territory. They lived in large communities, with town centers. They farmed and raised livestock.

Georgia Cherokee – Similar to the Creek, their nation was a confederacy of towns, each subordinate to supreme. They adopted the European lifestyle, and fought against the Creek with Andrew Jackson (1813-1814). When Gold was discovered and they were forced from their lands.

Georgia, U.S., and World History Events

Native American cultures in North America and interactions with early explorers

United States Indians:

Arctic (Inuit) – Term used as a general grouping of similar, indigenous people located in the areas of Greenland, Canada, and Alaska. These people are also known as Eskimos, and tend to be hunters and fishers.

Northwest (Kwakiutl) – Describes a set of indigenous people from the Pacific Northwest Coast. These people lived in cedar homes, and relied on the sea for most of their food.

Plateau (Nez Perce) – A set of indigenous people from the Pacific Northwest, more specifically the Columbia River Plateau. These people were migratory and traveled with the seasons.

Southwest (Hopi) – Indians who settled in what is now Arizona. They lived in adobe homes. They were expert farmers and their men also hunted.

Plains (Pawnee) – Indigenous people from the Great Plains Region; agricultural people who used horses for work and transportation. They lived in round earthen lodges.

Southeast (Seminole) – Originally from Florida, they were once members of the Creek Nation. They were on good terms with the Spanish and British. They lived in houses called chickees, which were made of wood and plaster with thatched roofs, and they were farmers.

Trail of Tears – was part of President Jackson's Indian Removal Act, which said that Native Americans should be moved west of the Mississippi. This was mainly the removal of the Cherokee from the state of Georgia and surrounding areas. During the years of 1838 to 1839, around 15,000 Cherokee were forced to travel more than 800 miles. Many of them died from sickness and hunger.

Georgia, U.S., and World History Events

Events, issues, and developments in history

Georgia History:

James Oglethorpe – Founder of the colony of Georgia, he wanted a place for those in debtors' prison. He negotiated with the Creek Indian tribe for the land.

Tomochichi – A 16th-century Creek leader and the head chief of Yamacrow, a town on the site of present day Savannah, Georgia. He is important because he wanted his people educated and was friends with the English.

Mary Musgrove – helped bridge the gap between Georgia settlers and the Creek. She married a former English indentured servant.

Sequoyah – developed the Cherokee alphabet. This changed the Cherokee into a literate nation.

Jackie Robinson – born in Cairo, Georgia. He was the first African American major league baseball player and went to the World Series.

Jimmy Carter – First president to come from Georgia, he was known for his leadership and active interest in human rights.

Exploration in North America by the Spanish, French, and English:

John Cabot – Italian navigator; discovered the North America mainland.

Vasco Nunez de Balboa – Spanish Explorer and conquistador; the first European to see the Pacific Ocean.

Juan Ponce De Leon – Spanish explorer; first European to set foot in Florida. He also discovered the Atlantic Gulf Stream and was constantly searching for the fountain of youth.

Christopher Columbus – Famous for discovering the New World, though he died believing he found the Indies.

Henry Hudson – English Sea Explorer and merchant; explored a prospective Northeast Passage to India.

Jacques Cartier – a French explorer who claimed what is now Canada for France.

Georgia, U.S., and World History Events

Strategies and resources for historical inquiry

Students must perform research to learn more about a given topic. In history, students research topics and present the information to the class. This is a good way for students to learn details about history-related events. Resources include the Internet, print, and primary.

Internet – The Internet is everywhere, and it has made its way into the classroom. It is used to bring in virtual field trips, weather, C-SPAN, videos, demonstrations, Google Earth, and web cams from international classrooms.

Print – In the world of electronic everything, it is important to provide plenty of materials in print. Students need tangible sources of information as well in order to provide a broad spectrum of information.

Primary, aka Original Source – This is a document or another source of information that was created at the time of study. The source has direct personal knowledge of the information or event.
Examples of primary sources:
- Original Documents – Letters, Manuscripts, interviews
- Creative Works – Novels, art, and music
- Artifacts – Pottery

Georgia, U.S., and World History Events

Events, issues, and developments in history

Colonial Life in America:
Colonial America consisted of three distinct regions: New England, Mid-Atlantic, and Southern.

	New England	Mid-Atlantic	Southern
States found in these areas	Massachusetts, Connecticut, Rhode Island, and New Hampshire	Pennsylvania, New York, New Jersey	Virginia, Maryland, North and South Carolina, Georgia
Culture and economic situation in these areas	Poorest region of the three – its rocky soil could not sustain farming for valuable export crops	Diverse cultural mixtures: Irish, English, Wales, German, Scots; these cultures did not always mesh well	These people came to the New World looking for economic gain, imported indentured servants, and lived in an area devoted to farming
Types of people in these areas	Artisans, farmers, Native Americans	Artisans, Native Americans	Land owners, artisans, farmers, indentured servants, slaves, Native Americans

Georgia, U.S., and World History Events

Questions to Recap:

1. The Civil Rights Act ensured _____ rights for African Americans.

2. Name two causes of World War II.

3. Which of the following people were important figures during the Civil War?
   - a. Ben Franklin
   - b. Abraham Lincoln
   - c. Robert E. Lee
   - d. John F. Kennedy
   - e. b and c
   - f. c and d

4. List the three distinct regions of Colonial America.

5. True or False: King George II was the king of France during World War I.

6. Two types of Georgia Indians are the:
   - a. Creek and Pawnee
   - b. Hopi and Seminole
   - c. Creek and Cherokee
   - d. Cherokee and Pawnee
   - e. Inuit and Seminole

7. Resources that students can use to find about more about history-related events include _____, _____, and _____.

8. Vasco Nunez de Balboa was the first European to see the _____.

1.) equal 2.) Japan was expanding, Italy wanted Ethiopia, Spanish Civil War, Hitler started expanding 3.) e 4.) New England, Mid-Atlantic, Southern 5.) False 6.) c 7.) Internet, Print, Primary 8.) Pacific Ocean

Geography
Basic concepts of geography

Geography: the study of locations and how living things and Earth's features are distributed.

The Six Essential Elements of Geography and Terms for Each Element:

The World in Spatial Terms:
This is the use of maps, tools, and technology to acquire processes and report information from a spatial perspective. As we move through a new area, we tend to mentally map out the area. For example, when we visit a new home, we map out the location of the restroom as the third door on the left.

Places and Regions:
This describes the physical and human characteristics of places. Different people, with their culture and experience, influence people's perceptions of places and regions.

Physical Systems:
These are the physical processes that shape the earth's surface: erosion, weathering, deposition, and natural disasters. It also includes the characteristics and distribution of ecosystems on the earth's surface.

Human Systems:
This describes the characteristics, distribution, and migration of human populations on the earth's surface and includes the interdependence of one region on another. It also describes the processes and patterns related to human settlement and how conflicts among people influence the division and control of earth's surface and resources.

Environment and Society:
This is how human actions modify the physical environment and, in turn, how the natural systems affect the humans. For example, people from the past in the New Orleans area diminished their natural swamps and built lakes and canals to divert water from here or there. This removed the region's natural defenses from storm surges. The result is neighborhood flooding.

The Uses of Geography:
This is how to apply geography to your needs. People shape the land – by building homes in hillsides, building dams, building roads, and destroying swampland to create fields for agriculture, digging ponds, and lakes.

Geography

Major physical and human-constructed features of the earth

Major Concepts of Geography: Location, movement of people, and interactions of people. Location is determined with cardinal directions and lines of longitude and latitude.

Latitude – drawn east to west; a specific line of latitude is the Equator; measures 'how far north or south'; Latitude = *fatitude*

- Longitude – drawn north to south; a specific line of longitude is the Prime Meridian, which measures how far east or west.

Geographical Regions and Major Rivers of Georgia:

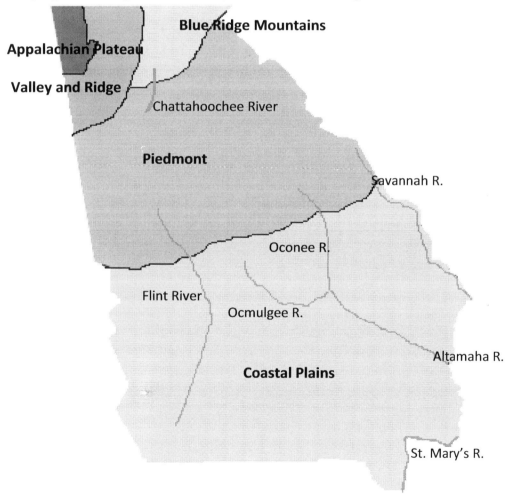

Geography

Major physical and human-constructed features of the earth

Major United States Rivers and Mountain Ranges:

Major Geographical Areas:

(Note – this picture is not to scale and is to be used only as a special guide to understand the general regions.)

Geography

Major physical and human-constructed features of the earth

Major Physical Features of the Earth:
- Mountains – stretch above the surrounding land.
- Valley – is a depression in the earth.
- Plains – are vast areas of flat land.
- Plateau – is a highland area, usually consisting of relatively flat land.
- Desert – is a region that receives very little precipitation (can be cold or hot); temperatures are usually extreme.
- Coast – is where a large body of water meets land.

Note: You should know the seven continents and the five oceans and their locations.
- Continents – Asia, Europe, Australia, N. America, S. America, Africa, and Antarctica.
- Oceans – Atlantic, Arctic, Pacific, Indian, and Southern.

Famous Man-Made Locations:
- New York City, NY – The city itself is an engineering marvel; the Statue of Liberty and Empire State Building are located there.
- Boston, MA – The location of Boston harbor, which was discovered by John Smith and had been filled along the edge to create more coast line.
- Philadelphia, PA – The location of Independence Hall as well as the Liberty Bell.
- Erie Canal – Man-made canal, which was the first route to connect trade between the Atlantic Ocean and the Great Lakes.

Geography

Physical systems and human systems

Geography can be divided into two main areas, human geography and physical geography. As humans, we interact daily with physical systems to make money through agriculture and mining and to develop land for homes and business.

Major factors that influenced these systems were the Agricultural Revolution and the Industrial Revolution.

Geography
Maps, globes, and other geographic tools

Types of Maps:
- Political – shows lines defining counties.
- Physical – show landmarks such as oceans, lakes, rivers, and mountains.
- Topographic – a detailed graphic representation of natural features on the ground; shows how high or low an area is.
- Resource – depicts available resources and locations.

Tools on Maps:
- Compass Rose – found on the map; shows direction of north, south, east, and west.
- Legend – provides information needed to understand symbols used on the map.
- Map Scale – usually found on bottom edge of the map; shows how distance is represented.
  Example: 1 inch = 50 miles

Geography
Strategies and resources for geographic inquiry

To read a map, students must have knowledge of the map. Students must know the type of map and understand how to use the tools on the map. Reading maps takes practice like all other skills. Repetitive practice is essential for reading a map.

Geography

Questions to Recap:

1. The Compass Rose tool on a map shows _____.

2. An element of geography that describes how human actions affect the natural environment and how the natural systems affect humans is called _____.

3. Name two geographical regions of Georgia.

4. Which of the following are major natural physical features of the earth:
    a. Plateaus
    b. Valleys
    c. Erie Canal
    d. Coast

1.) direction 2.) environment and society 3.) Appalachian Plateau, Valley and Ridge, Blue Ridge Mountains, Piedmont, Coastal Plains
4.) a, b, d

Government and Civics

Functions of government and the basic principles of the U.S. government

Functions of the Government (found in the Preamble of the Constitution):

1. To Form a More Perfect Union – The government will be fair throughout the union, from state to state and city to city.
2. Establish Justice – It is the government's job to protect people who follow the rules and punish those who do not.
3. Ensure Domestic Tranquility – You are entitled to a tranquil and quiet life.
4. Provide for the Common Defense – The government protects innocent life and provides protection from external threats (with military).
5. Promote the General Welfare – The government's job is to ensure that everyone is represented fairly, regardless of class or social standing.
6. Secure the Blessings of Liberty to Ourselves and our Posterity – Blessings are from God, not a privilege granted by government. Blessings are life, liberty, and property – the government doesn't provide these; it only protects them.

Government and Civics

Roles and powers of the branches of government

Structure and Power of the Government Branches:
Legislative Branch – This branch is made up of Congress and the government agencies that provide support to Congress.
Congress – Its job is to write bills, debate them, and pass them, though the president has the final say on whether the bill becomes law. It can also make laws related to trade (between states, or between the U.S. and other countries), taxes, borrowing and printing money, and it can declare war on other countries.

- **House of Representatives** – The number of representatives a state has depends on the population of the state. They have the job of creating bills related to taxes. They also have the power to decide if a government official can be tried before the Senate.
- **Senate** – The number of Senate members per state is two, no matter what the population is. They can hold trials for government officials. They also have the power to make decisions about treaties and individuals the president wants to hire. The Vice President is the president of the Senate.

Government and Civics

Roles and powers of the branches of government

Structure and Power of the Government Branches (cont'd.):

Judicial Branch:
This is the court system, and the Supreme Court is the highest court in the United States.
The Supreme Court – has nine members called Justices. The leader is known as the Chief Justice. The members are all appointed by presidents; however, they must be approved by the Senate. Different from most other political officials, they have their jobs for life or until they retire or resign. In order for a Justice to be removed from the Supreme Court, they must be impeached by the House of Representatives and convicted by the Senate.

Executive Branch:
This branch insures that the laws of the U.S. are followed. This branch is made of the President, the Vice President, and independent agencies and departments that aid the President, such as the President's Cabinet.
President – The leader of the U.S. and in command of the military. The President is called the Commander-in-Chief.
Vice President – The president of the Senate, the Vice President has the responsibility to become the President of the United States if anything happens to the President.
President's Cabinet – People chosen by the President and approved by the Senate. They give the President advice about different matters like education, defense, homeland security, and money.

- **Secretary of Education** – This cabinet member's job is to make decisions addressing the needs for American education.
- **Secretary of Defense** – This cabinet member's job is to oversee all branches of the military.
- **Secretary of Homeland Security** – This cabinet member's job is to work to prevent terrorist attacks within the United States and to minimize the damage from natural disasters.
- **Secretary of the Treasury** – This cabinet member's job is to supervise tax collection and the printing of money.

Government and Civics

The roles and interrelationships among national, state, and local government

Three Levels of Government:
- National – President, Congress, Supreme Court.
- State – Governor, state legislature, state court.
- Local – Mayor, county commissioner or city council, city/county court.

Three Branches in Each:
- Executive – President, governor, mayor.
- Legislative – Congress, state legislature, city council.
- Judicial – Supreme Court, state court, city/county court.

Government and Civics

Declaration of Independence, the U.S. Constitution, and the Bill of Rights

Declaration of Independence – Represented the official step towards separation from Great Britain; written by Thomas Jefferson during the Second Continental Congress.

U.S. Constitution – Written after it was decided that the Articles of Confederation were not working. The first draft was written in 1787 by the Constitutional Convention.

Bill of Rights – First ten amendments introduced by James Madison; added to the U.S. Constitution because 'they' felt the Constitution did not protect certain freedoms. Some of the freedoms the Bill of Rights protects are: freedom of religion, assembly, speech, press, the right to keep and bear arms and protection for those accused of crimes.
1. Freedom of speech, religion, press, petition, and assembly
2. Right to bear arms, and militia
3. Quartering of soldiers
4. Warrants and searches
5. Individual debt and double jeopardy
6. Speedy trial, witness, and accusations
7. Right for a jury trial
8. Bail and fines
9. Existence of other rights for the people
10. Power reserved to the states and people

Government and Civics

The rights and responsibilities of U.S. citizenship, Rights of Americans

The rights of Americans are laid out by the Bill of Rights (listed earlier in the book, page 86).

Rights and Responsibilities of U.S. Citizens:
- Obey laws
- Pay taxes
- Jury duty
- Serve as a witness
- Register for the draft
- Voting

Government and Civics

Strategies and resources for inquiry related to government and civics

In today's fast paced, instant access world, teachers can pull up C-SPAN so that students can see the government in action. Teachers can pull up information on the government; the internet has limitless resources. There are also tools such as Google Earth, where students can visit the Parthenon in Athens, Washington D.C., and many other locations.

Questions to Recap:

1. What are the three branches of the U.S. government?

2. The following are all rights and responsibilities of U.S. citizens, except:
    a. Voting
    b. Pay taxes
    c. Obeying laws
    d. All of the above

3. The number of representatives each state has is _____ and the number of senators each state has is _____.

1.) Legislative, Judicial, Executive 2.) d 3.) based on population, two

Economics

Recognizing basic economic concepts and the purposes and functions of currency

Goods and Services:
- Goods – are things you can use or consume, such as food or shoes.
- Services – are things someone does for you, such as a haircut or lawn care.

Scarcity – is how little of something is available; the amount of a supply.

Supply and Demand:
- Supply – is the amount of something that is available.
- Demand – is the amount of something that is needed.

If the supply is greater than the demand, the cost goes down. If the demand is greater than the supply, the cost increases.

Needs and Wants:
- Needs – are things you have to have, such as food, shelter, clothing, and medicine.
- Wants – are things you would like to have.

Opportunity Cost – is best explained as when an item is unavailable and you have to choose an alternative. For example, if you have an apple everyday with your lunch but when you go to the store they are out, instead you'll buy peaches.

Productivity – is the amount of output from a production process.

Economics

Recognizing basic economic concepts and the purposes and functions of currency

Trade – is important to the success of any civilization. It is the exchange of goods and services between countries. Most nations produce goods that other countries need. Trade creates dependency.

Trade among Regions: Trade is affected by economy, culture, and politics. Also, different regions of the world have access to different resources provided by that region.

Currency – refers to tangible currency (dollar, coins, or banknotes). Currency is the basis of the economic world. In a perfect society a country's currency is backed by gold and silver; this is where money gets its value.

Economics – is not simply money; it is the concept of how business and money work together.

Economics

The roles and interactions of consumers and producers in the U.S. economy

Consumer – The user of goods and services to satisfy wants and needs. As a consumer you have responsibilities, such as shopping carefully, asking questions, and being informed.

Producers – are the people or companies that make and supply goods and services. As a producer you have the responsibility to the consumer to provide quality goods at an affordable rate.

Economics

The basic structure of the U.S. economy and interactions

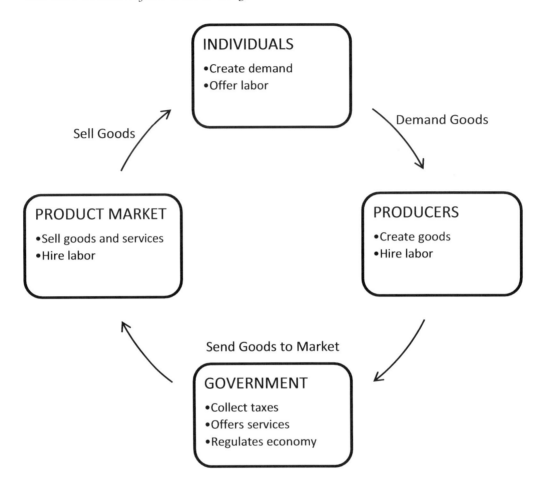

The U.S. economy interacts with other nations in the same way we interact with local stores.

Economics

Identifying the functions of private business, banks, and the government

Businesses provide goods – these goods provide revenue or money. This money fills banks and the government taxes that money. The money collected is called tax and that is used to provide goods and services.

Economics

Skills necessary to make reasoned and responsible financial decisions

Saver – Savers avoid wasting resources and are an important component of the banking system, because their money in the bank makes it possible for the borrower to borrow money.

Borrower – has a responsibility to repay the amount borrowed following the repayment guidelines outlined by the lender.

Questions to Recap:

1. If demand is _____ than supply, the cost increases.

2. What is opportunity cost?

3. _____ is the exchange of goods and services between countries.

1.) greater 2.) is choosing a different item 3.) trade

PART 2 Test 2 (Test Code 002)

Mathematics:

This section consists of 25 multiple choice questions and one essay question. Please refer to the GACE website for practice questions.

Science:

This section consists of 20 multiple choice questions and one essay question. The science sections include: characteristics of science, earth science, physical science, and life science. Please refer to the GACE website for practice questions.

Health, Physical Education, and The Arts:

This section consists of 15 multiple choice questions and NO essay question. Please refer to the GACE website for practice questions.

Mathematics

This section is organized according to the frameworks available in PDF format from the GACE website www.gace.nesinc.com. There are five objectives for this section making it the longest section in Test II.

Items in this section:
- ☑ Exploring Mathematics and Solving Problems
- ☑ Numbers and Mathematical Operations
- ☑ Geometry
- ☑ Algebra
- ☑ Data Analysis

NOTE: It is important to be familiar with basic math because calculators are not permitted during this exam.

Exploring Mathematics and Solving Problems
Strategies for solving problems in math

Relevant Information:
When solving problems in math, it is important to identify the relevant information. For example, in the following word problem, Emily is going to the store to buy supplies for a surprise birthday party. She needs eggs, oil, cake mix, frosting, candles, balloons, plates, and napkins. She has $100 for these supplies. Take a look at her receipt to decide if she has enough money. The total is $91.38, so, yes she has enough money.

Fresh Farm Eggs (dozen)	1 @ 5.45 = $5.45
Vegetable Oil	1 @ 8.00 = $8.00
Higgins Chocolate Cake Mix	2 @ 2.22 = $4.44
Higgins Chocolate Frosting	2 @ 1.50 = $3.00
Magic Candles	1 @ 6.65 = $6.65
Birthday Balloons, 12 count	2 @ 9.92 = $19.84
Blue Party Plates, 8 count	6 @ 4.00 = $24.00
Blue Party Napkins, 12 count	4 @ 5.10 = $20.40
Total	

Deciding relevant information – The items on the list are insignificant as are the use of the items. Also, the cost per item is not needed either. We simply need the total to decide if Emily had enough money.

Simplifying:
Simplifying in math is an important process. We simplify fractions and equations to make the information easier to understand.

Fraction Example:

$$\frac{49}{343} \text{ simplifys or reduces to } \frac{7}{49} \text{ and further reduces to } \frac{1}{7}$$

Equation Example:

$$3x + 7 - 12x + 3y - 2 - 11y$$
$$-9x + 7 + 3y - 2 - 11y$$
$$-9x + 5 + 3y - 11y$$
$$-9x + 5 - 8y$$

Estimation:
This is taught so students can calculate information faster. This is also a helpful skill when teaching and carrying out mental math.

Exploring Mathematics and Solving Problems
Language and vocabulary in math

Words in Math:
If you struggle with the words in math problems, go through and make a few note cards with these words. It will help you quickly identify the words used in word problems, and give you more confidence with word problems in general.

Operation	Words
Addition	Sum, Together, Total of, Added to, Increased, Increased by, More, More than
Subtraction	Minus, Less, Decreased by, Difference between, Less than, Fewer than
Multiplication	Times, Multiplied by, Of, Product of, By, Increased or Decreased by a Factor of (x)
Division	Per, Out of, Ratio of, Split, Quotient
Equals	Is, Are, Was, Were, Will be, Gives, Yields, For, Sells for, Sold for

Complete the Following: (answers on page 142)

1.) The opposite of adding 5 is _____.

2.) The sum of 7 and 27 _____.

3.) The number of children split evenly among 4 parents_____.

Exploring Mathematics and Solving Problems

Materials, models, and methods, and technologies used to explore mathematical concepts

Mathematics can be explored in a number of ways. Concepts are taught and reinforced with a careful balance of materials, models, and technologies. Common materials, or manipulatives, are used throughout math instruction. Also, strategies such as models are used to introduce and reinforce concepts. They are used to help students create mental images of number or mathematical concepts.

Resources available in today's word are almost limitless. In mathematics, we use manipulatives, texts, spinners, number cubes, software, the internet, handheld calculators, and spreadsheets to bring meaning and understanding to mathematical concepts.

Manipulatives – Teaching tools that are hands-on items used to give more meaning to content. They include, but are not limited to, models, tools, and other devices used to understand concepts.

Manipulatives are a vital component of any math classroom. Examples include Popsicle sticks for counting, fraction pieces, three-dimensional objects, and nets. These are used to bring meaning to numbers. Without manipulatives to represent the intangible, math is sometimes hard to understand. Manipulative use starts with physical quantities of things. Teachers then move to demonstrating principles of addition and subtraction with tangible items.

Physical Models, or Representations – Teaching tools that are tangible representations of "things." In math there are many complex ideas. Models and representations show these things in a concrete or visible way. This is done with the use of manipulatives, graphs, and software. Examples of physical models are geometric figures, nets, and abacus.

Exploring Mathematics and Solving Problems
Connections in math

We will consistently tell and teach our students that they will encounter math nearly every day of their lives. This can be an empty and meaningless statement if the teacher does not back it up with real life examples. It is important to make connections to students' lives with content. This makes the information more meaningful for the students. Information that is meaningful to the students is more readily remembered.

Numbers and Mathematical Operations
Concepts of quantities, comparing, order, estimate, and rounding

Comparing Numbers – Numbers are compared either by size or by their distance from zero on the number line. The numbers to the right of the zero are the positive numbers and the numbers to the left of the zero are the negative numbers. Symbols are used to represent the relationships between numbers.

Symbol	Meaning
<	Less than; this can be remembered because the sign looks like an 'L'
>	Greater than
=	Equal to
≠	Not equal
≤	Less than or Equal to
≥	Greater than or Equal to

Comparing Whole Numbers: (answers on page 142)

1.)   114 ( ) 165   2.)   193 ( ) 139   3.)   6011 ( ) 6101

Numbers and Mathematical Operations

Concepts of quantities, comparing, order, estimate, and rounding

Comparing Money and Decimals – To compare decimal numbers and money, we consider numbers that use place value and decimal points to show tenths, hundredths or any value less than 1.

Place Value

1	2	3	4	5	6	7	.	8	9	1
Million	Hundred thousand	Ten thousand	One thousand	One hundred	Tens	Ones		Tenths	Hundredths	Thousandths

Comparing Decimals – To compare decimals, we evaluate the numbers that come before the decimal point. If they are equal, we evaluate the numbers after the decimal point until we see a difference. Once there is a difference, the largest number represents the larger complete number.

Example: 156.023 and 156.032; the numbers are the same up to the hundredths place, and 2 is less than 3; therefore, 156.023 < 156.032.
Example: 865,456.258 and 865,456.248; the numbers are the same up to the hundredths place, and 5 is greater than 4; therefore, 865,456.258 > 865,456.248.

Percents: Parts per 100; the symbol for percent is %.
To compare percents, use whole number and decimal rules.

Comparing Decimals and Percents: (answers on page 142)

1.) $1.21 ( ) $1.12   2.)   0.90% ( ) 0.86%   3.)   1.001 ( ) .0001

Numbers and Mathematical Operations

Concepts of quantities, comparing, order, estimate, and rounding

Fractions:
Fractions are representations of pieces of numbers or groups; they can be negative or positive. Fractions are composed of numerators (top of the fraction) and denominators (bottom of the fraction).

To Compare Fractions –
use greater than (>) or less than (<) symbols.

$$\frac{3}{5} < \frac{4}{5}$$ Numerator / Denominator

When the **denominators of the fractions are the same**, the larger fraction will be the one that has the largest numerator.

In the above problem, the fractions have the same denominator but different numerators. This means that 3/5 is less than 4/5.

When the **denominators are different**, you must cross multiply, or get the cross product. The first cross-multiple is the product of the first numerator multiplied by the second denominator. The second cross-multiple is the product of the second numerator multiplied by the first denominator. Once you have your results, compare the products. If the results are equal, the fractions are equal. If the first result is larger, the first fraction is larger. And, if the second result is larger, the second fraction is larger.

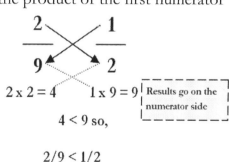

$2 \times 2 = 4 \qquad 1 \times 9 = 9$ Results go on the numerator side

$4 < 9$ so,

$2/9 < 1/2$

Fractions can also be compared using illustrations and number lines.
Example of pictures:

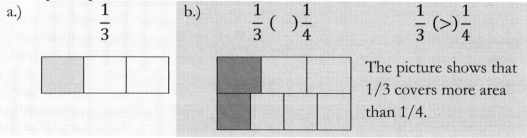

The picture shows that 1/3 covers more area than 1/4.

Numbers and Mathematical Operations
Concepts of quantities, comparing, order, estimate, and rounding

Number Line:

Example: $\frac{1}{4}\ (\ )\ \frac{3}{4} \rightarrow \frac{1}{4}\ (<)\ \frac{3}{4}$

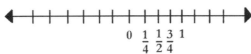

Order:
It is important that students understand how to organize a group of numbers from least to greatest or greatest to least.

Put the following in order from greatest to least:

Example: $\mathbf{5.33, 1\frac{1}{3}, 3.33, 2} \rightarrow 5.33, 3.33, 2, 1\frac{1}{3}$

Example: $\mathbf{1\frac{7}{8}, 1\frac{1}{2}, 2\frac{5}{7}, 1\frac{2}{3}} \rightarrow 2\frac{5}{7}, 1\frac{7}{8}, 1\frac{2}{3}, 1\frac{1}{2}$

Put the following in order from least to greatest:

Example $-\ \mathbf{-23, 15, -62, -.02} \rightarrow -62, -23, -.02, 15$

Put the following in order from least to greatest: (answers on page 142)

1.) $\frac{1}{2}, \frac{5}{7}, \frac{1}{3}, \frac{4}{5}$
2.) $0.002, 1.02, 0.2, 0.02$
3.) $70\%,\ 0.11, 0.25\%, 0$

Estimation:
Estimation is a powerful mathematical tool that will be used throughout a student's life. This is very important when teaching mental math.

Things to estimate: large quantities, distances, and data.

We use estimation to find an answer that is close to the exact answer.
Estimation uses rounding to make calculations easier.
Estimation words: about, close to, around, between.

Example: A way to teach/introduce this would be to hold up a jar of jelly beans and ask students to guess how many jelly beans there are.

Numbers and Mathematical Operations
Concepts of quantities, comparing, order, estimate, and rounding

Rounding – This is the process of reducing the digits. Most of the time, we round to the nearest tenth, which makes mental math easier.
   Example: 67 is larger than 65 and closer to 70, so we round up to 70
   Example: 62 is smaller than 65 and closer to 60, so we round down to 60

Example: Every season, there are 42 new episodes produced for one of the late night talk shows. If a person does eight seasons, estimate how many shows there will be.
Estimate: 8×42, round 42 to the nearest ten to make the calculation easier. So, $8 \times 40 = 320$, or around 320 shows.

This is important when teaching mental math skills to your students. It will be essential that they can do some calculations in their heads.

Example: Amy bought 5 notebooks at $3.61 each. She estimated that she would spend $15. Is her estimate appropriate?
Answer: No, because the 3.61 should be rounded up to 4 and $5 \times 4 = 20$.

Rounding Problems: (answers on page 142)
Directions – Round to the nearest tenths place:

1.) 273.46

2.) 1.61

3.) 57.076

Directions – Round to the nearest hundreds place:

4.) 5,378

5.) 192

6.) 11,678

7.) 4,231

Numbers and Mathematical Operations
Concepts of place value, prime numbers, multiples, and factors

Place Value:

1	2	3	4	5	6	7	.	8	9	1
Million	Hundred thousand	Ten thousand	One thousand	One hundred	Tens	Ones		Tenths	Hundredths	Thousandths

Number Theory – The branch of math that studies the properties of natural numbers; also known as positive integers.

Prime Number – is a natural number that is greater than 1 and only has 2 factors: 1 and itself.
    Examples: 2, 3, 5, 7, 11, 13, 17, 19, 23, 29 . . .

Composite Numbers – are natural numbers that are greater than 1 and are not prime numbers. They are divisible by more than 1 and themselves.
    Examples: 4 is divisible by 1, 2, and 4

Factors – are natural numbers that divides exactly into another number, or a whole that is multiplied with another number to make a third number.
The factors of 36 are: 1, 2, 3, 4, 6, 9, 12, 18, and 36.
    Examples: 2x4=8   2 and 4 are factors of 8
                      3x5=15   3 and 5 are factors of 15

A special kind of factor is called the **Greatest Common Factor**. This is the largest number that will divide into two numbers two or more times exactly.

Find the **greatest common factor** of 9, 12, and 18.
9   1, 3, 9
12   1, 2, 3, 4, 6, 12
18   1, 2, 3, 6, 9, 18
3 is the common factor

Numbers and Mathematical Operations

Concepts of place value, prime numbers, multiples, and factors

Find the greatest common factor of 12, 20, and 24.
12   1, 2, 3, 4, 6, 12
20   1, 2, 4, 5, 10, 20
24   1, 2, 3, 4, 6, 8, 12, 24
4 is the common factor

Find the greatest common factor of 14, 21, and 28.
14   1, 2, 7, 14
21   1, 3, 7, 21
28   1, 2, 4, 7, 14, 28
7 is the common factor.

Find the GCF's for the following numbers: (answers on page 142)

1.)   24, 36

2.)   18, 36, 42

3.)   12, 56, 60

4.)   9, 63

Multiple – The product of the number and any other whole number; they are the result of multiplying by a whole number.

Examples: Multiples of 4 – 4, 8, 12, 16, 20, 24, 28, 32
Multiples of 5 – 5, 10, 15, 20, 25, 30, 35, 40

Multiples of 4:

1x4	2x4	3x4	4x4	5x4	6x4	7x4
4	8	12	16	20	24	28

Numbers and Mathematical Operations

Concepts of place value, prime numbers, multiples, and factors

Percent's:

Parts of a whole (100). When percent's are written as words, they are written: "this" is "some percent" of "that," or they can be written as "%" over "100" = "is" over "of."

$\frac{\%}{100} = \frac{is}{of}$ Using this equation, we can use cross multiplication and find any component missing in a percentage problem. In this equation, the "100" does not change.

Example:
What is 25% of 80?

Formula: Equation:

$\frac{\%}{100} = \frac{is}{of} \rightarrow \frac{25\%}{100} = \frac{x}{80} \rightarrow 25 \times 80 = 100 \times X \rightarrow 2000 = 100x$

$\rightarrow \frac{2000}{100} = \frac{100x}{100} \rightarrow 20 = x \rightarrow$ so 20 *is* 25% *of* 80

This is used for calculating tips, sale prices, taxes, and much more.

Solve the Following: (answers on page 143)

1.) What is 20% of 60?

2.) 0.2 is 10% of what number?

3.) What percent of 300 is 6?

4.) 4.8% of 32 is what number?

Numbers and Mathematical Operations

Equivalent forms of common fractions, decimal fractions, and percentages

Decimal to a Fraction:
Step 1: Write down the decimals divided by 1
Step 2: Multiply both top and bottom by 100 for every number after the decimal point
Step 3: Simplify

Problem: Write 0.75 as a fraction.

1.) Write down: $\frac{0.75}{1}$

2.) Multiply both the top and bottom by 100: $\frac{0.75}{1} \times \frac{100}{100} = \frac{75}{100}$

3.) Simplify: $\frac{75}{100} = \frac{3}{4}$

Convert the following decimals to fractions: (answers on page 143)

1.) 0.25

2.) 0.80

3.) 0.65

Fraction to Decimal:
Step 1: Divide numerator by denominator
Step 2: Place the decimal

Problem: Write $\frac{3}{4}$ as a decimal

$$\frac{3}{4} = 4\overline{)30} \begin{array}{c} .75 \\ -28 \\ 20 \\ -20 \\ 0 \end{array} = .75$$

Convert the following fractions to decimals: (answers on page 144)

1.) $\frac{1}{3}$

2.) $\frac{5}{6}$

Numbers and Mathematical Operations

Equivalent forms of common fractions, decimal fractions, and percentages

Percent to a Fraction
Step 1: Write down the percent divided by 100
Step 2: Reduce

Problem: Write 75% as a fraction
    Step 1: Start by placing the percent over 100
    Step 2: Then reduce or simplify.

$$\frac{75}{100} = now\ simplify\ the\ fraction;\ 25\ will\ go\ into\ each = \frac{3}{4}$$

Convert the following percent to fraction: (answers on page 144)
    1.) 25%

    2.) 45%

    3.) 30%

Fraction to a Percent
This is sometimes the hardest to complete because it has the most steps.
Step 1: Set up fraction as an equation fraction = x/100
Step 2: Solve for x by cross multiplying
Step 3: Attach a % sign to the answer for "x"

$$\frac{3}{4} \rightarrow \frac{3}{4} = \frac{x}{100}$$

$$\frac{3}{4} \times \frac{x}{100}$$

$$4x = 300$$

$$x = 75$$

$$so, \frac{3}{4} = 75\%$$

Show work:
```
       7 5
   4 )3 0 0
     -2 8
      ───
       2 0
     - 2 0
      ───
         0
```

Convert the following fractions to percent: (answers on page 144)

    1.) $\frac{1}{2}$ 2.) $\frac{2}{3}$ 3.) $\frac{4}{5}$

Numbers and Mathematical Operations

Equivalent forms of common fractions, decimal fractions, and percentages

Decimals to Percents:

To convert a decimal to a percent, simply move the decimal point two places to the right, insert zeros as placeholders if needed, and attach the % sign.

Examples:

.15 = 15. = 15%

.849 = 84.9 = 84.9%

Convert the following decimals to percent's: (answers on page 144)

   1.) 4.5   2.) .259   3.) 45.6

Percents to Decimals:

To convert a percent to a decimal, remove the % sign and move the decimal point two places to the left; you may need to insert zeros as placeholders.

Examples:

76% = 76. = .76

54.9% = 54.9 = .549

Convert the following percent's to decimals: (answers on page 144)

   1.) 22%   2.) 7.1%   3.) 19.6%

Numbers and Mathematical Operations

Properties of numbers and the number system

Number Properties:

Properties	Defined	Examples	Notes and Additions
Commutative	Means that the order of the numbers does not affect the outcome	$2 + 3 = 3 + 2$ $6 + 8 = 8 + 6$	This property does not work with subtraction
Associative	Means that grouping does not affect the outcome	$(1+2)+3 = 1+(2+3)$	Works only in addition and multiplication
Distributive	Is simply a concept which will allow you to simplify a number being multiplied by a set of parenthesis	$3(3+4) = 3(3)+3(4)$	
Identity	Any number added to 0 gives the original number	$3+0 = 3$ $21+0 = 21$	Property for the addition of 0
	Any number multiplied by 1 gives the original number	$21 \times 1 = 21$ $888 \times 1 = 888$	Property for the multiplication of 1
Zero	When a number is multiplied by 0, the number equals 0	$4 \times 0 = 0$	

Numbers and Mathematical Operations

Calculations with whole numbers, decimals, and fractions

Operations with Whole Numbers:

Addition	Subtraction
$1 + 1 = 2$	$5 - 2 = 3$
$\begin{array}{r} 1 \\ 38 \\ +26 \\ \hline 64 \end{array}$	$\begin{array}{r} 2\,9 \\ \cancel{3}\,\cancel{0}\,2 \\ -1\,7\,3 \\ \hline 1\,2\,9 \end{array}$
Multiplication	**Division**
$2 \times 9 = 18$ $\quad\quad \begin{array}{r} 27 \\ \times 22 \\ \hline 54 \\ +540 \\ \hline 594 \end{array}$ $\begin{array}{r} 7 \\ \times 4 \\ \hline 28 \end{array}$	$12 \div 3 = 4$ or $3\overline{)12} \atop \underline{-12} \atop 0$ or $\dfrac{12}{3} = 4$

Operations with Fractions:

Addition	
Rules or Steps	If the fractions have the same denominators, add the numerator and carry over the denominator. If the fractions have different denominators - Find the least common denominator. - Write equivalent fractions using the new denominator. - Add the fractions. - Simplify or reduce if needed.
Examples	Make sure the denominators of the fractions are the same! $\dfrac{1}{4} + \dfrac{1}{4}$ Add top (numerator) put the answer over the same denominators $\dfrac{1+1}{4} = \dfrac{2}{4}$ Problem: $\dfrac{1}{3} + \dfrac{1}{6}$ Different denominators $\dfrac{1}{3} + \dfrac{1}{6} \rightarrow \dfrac{(2)1}{(2)3} + \dfrac{1}{6} = \dfrac{(2+1)}{6} = \dfrac{3}{6} = \dfrac{1}{2}$

Numbers and Mathematical Operations

Calculations with whole numbers, decimals, and fractions

Subtraction	
Rules or Steps	*Addition and subtraction have the same steps; the only difference is the actual addition and subtraction.* If the fractions have the same denominators, subtract the numerator and carry over the denominator. If the fractions have different denominators, - Find the least common denominator. - Write equivalent fractions using the new denominator. - Subtract the fractions. - Simplify or reduce if needed.
Examples	**With like denominators subtract numerators and carry over denominators.** $$\frac{3}{4} - \frac{1}{4} = \frac{(3-1)}{4} = \frac{2}{4} = \frac{1}{2}$$ Same as addition $\quad \frac{1}{2} - \frac{1}{6} \rightarrow \frac{(3)1}{(3)2} - \frac{1}{6} = \frac{(3-1)}{6} = \frac{2}{6} = \frac{1}{3}$

Multiplication	
Rules or Steps	Fraction x Fraction: This is easier than addition and subtraction; simply multiply the numerators and the denominators, and then simplify.
	$$\frac{4}{7} \times \frac{1}{2} = \frac{4 \times 1}{7 \times 2} = \frac{4}{14} = \frac{2}{7}$$
Rules or Steps	Fraction x Whole Number: Write the whole number as an improper fraction with a denominator of 1 Then multiply as fractions.
Example	$$4 \times \frac{3}{5} \rightarrow \frac{4}{1} \times \frac{3}{5} = \frac{4 \times 3}{1 \times 5} = \frac{12}{5} \text{ or } 2\frac{2}{5}$$

Numbers and Mathematical Operations

Calculations with whole numbers, decimals, and fractions

Division	
Rules or Steps	Multiply the number by the reciprocal of the fraction. - Turn/flip the second fraction; this is now the reciprocal - Multiply across - Simplify
Examples	$\frac{1}{2} \div \frac{1}{6} = \frac{1}{2} \times \frac{6}{1} \{flipped\} \frac{1 \times 6}{2 \times 1} = \frac{6}{2} = 3$

Solve the following: (answers on page 145)

1.) $\frac{2}{3} \div \frac{5}{6}$ 2.) $-\frac{1}{7} \times \frac{7}{10}$ 3.) $\frac{2}{3} + \frac{5}{9}$ 4.) $\frac{7}{8} \div 6$

5.) $\frac{2}{3} \times \frac{7}{8}$ 6.) $\frac{9}{10} - 5$ 7.) $\frac{5}{12} - \frac{1}{9}$ 8.) $\frac{7}{8} + \frac{1}{20}$

Numbers and Mathematical Operations
Calculations with whole numbers, decimals, and fractions

Exponents:
These are used to represent repetitious multiplication of the same number such as $2 \times 2 \times 2 \times 2 \times 2 \times 2$ which is written 2^6. Where 2 is the base and 6 is the exponent or the number of times 2 is multiplied by itself. This is also used in scientific notation to represent very large numbers and very small numbers.

Examples:

Identify the base and the exponent in the following 3^5.	What does 4^3 mean?	What is 5^4?
3^5 base 3, exponent 5	4^3 $4 \times 4 \times 4$ 16×4 64	5^4 $5 \times 5 \times 5 \times 5$ $25 \times 5 \times 5$ 25×25 625

Examples with negative exponents and fractions:

What is 2^{-4}?	What is 3^{-3}?	$(\frac{2}{3})^3$
2^{-4} $\dfrac{1}{2 \times 2 \times 2 \times 2}$ $\dfrac{1}{4 \times 2 \times 2}$ $\dfrac{1}{8 \times 2}$ $\dfrac{1}{16}$	3^{-3} $\dfrac{1}{3 \times 3 \times 3}$ $\dfrac{1}{9 \times 3}$ $\dfrac{1}{27}$	$(\frac{2}{3})^3$ $\dfrac{2}{3} \times \dfrac{2}{3} \times \dfrac{2}{3}$ $\dfrac{4}{6} \times \dfrac{2}{3}$ $\dfrac{8}{18}$ or $\dfrac{4}{9}$

Complete the Following: (answers on page 146)

1.) Identify the base and the exponent in the following 5^3.

2.) What is 3^4?

3.) What is 4^5?

4.) What is 3^{-4}?

5.) What is 2^{-3}?

6.) $(\frac{1}{2})^3$

Numbers and Mathematical Operations
Calculations with whole numbers, decimals, and fractions

Operations with Decimals:

Addition	Subtraction
1.452 + 1.3	1.1 − 0.03
Line up decimals 1.452 +1.3	Line up decimals 1.1 −0.03
Hold places with zeros 1.452 +1.300	Fill places with zeros 1.10 −0.03
Add 1.452 +1.300 2.752	Subtract 1.1̸0¹⁰ −0.03 1.07
Multiplication	**Division**
0.03 × 1.1	Decimal by a whole number 9.1 by 7 divide 1st with '.'
Multiply without '.' 3 × 11 = 33	$\begin{array}{r} 13 \\ 7\overline{)91} \\ -7 \\ \hline 21 \\ -21 \end{array}$ then put in '.' $\begin{array}{r} 1.3 \\ 7\overline{)9.1} \end{array}$
0.03 has two decimal places and 1.1 has one, so the answer will have three decimal places	Whole number by a decimal move decimal over
Answer 0.033	6.625 ÷ 0.52, 52)662.5

Solve the following operations with decimals: (answers on page 146)
  1.) 32.35 + 1.2
  2.) 2.7 − 0.04
  3.) 10.232 − 1.78
  4.) 32.22 × 7.5
  5.) 7.2 ÷ 4
  6.) $\dfrac{7.231}{0.12}$

Numbers and Mathematical Operations

Calculations with whole numbers, decimals, and fractions

Operations with Integers:

Addition	
With the same sign: Add the absolute value Give the result the same sign	$2 + 3 = 5$ $(-8) + (-2) = -(8 + 2) = -10$ $(-12) + (-38) = -(12 + 38) = -50$
With the opposite signs: Take the absolute values Subtract the smaller from the larger Take the sign of the number with the larger absolute value	$8 + (-3) = 8 - 3 = 5$ $8 + (-12) = 8 - 12 = -9$ $-22 + 11 = -11$

Subtraction	
Subtracting integers is the same as adding the opposite.	$8 - 4 = 8 + (-4) = 4$ $15 - (-5) = 15 + 5 = 20$ $-10 - 8 = -10 + (-8) = -18$ $-12 - (-20) = -12 + (20) = 8$

Multiplication		
Rules and Steps	With multiplication, multiply the absolute value the numbers represent, then use the following rule to decide the sign.	$(+) \times (+) = (+)$ $(-) \times (-) = (+)$ $(+) \times (-) = (-)$ $(-) \times (+) = (-)$
Example	$4 \times (-4) = \|4x4\| = \|16\| = -16$ (because + x - = -) $-4 \times (-4) = \|4x4\| = \|16\| = 16$ (because - x - = +) $4 \times (-4) \times 4 = \|4x4x4\| = \|64\| = -64$ (+ x - x + = -) $4 \times (-4) \times (-4) = \|4x4x4\| = \|64\| = 64$ (+ x - x - = +)	

Numbers and Mathematical Operations

Calculations with whole numbers, decimals, and fractions

Division		
Rules and Steps	Same as multiplication; divide the absolute value the numbers represent, then use the following rule to decide the sign.	$(+) \div (+) = (+)$ $(-) \div (-) = (+)$ $(+) \div (-) = (-)$ $(-) \div (+) = (-)$
Example	$16 \div (-4) = \|16 \div 4\| = \|4\| = -4$ (because + x - = -) $-16 \div (-4) = \|16 \div 4\| = \|4\| = 4$ (because - x - = +) $12 \div (-2) \div 3 = \|12 \div 2 \div 3\| = \|2\| = -2$ (+ x - x + = -) $12 \div (-2) \div (-3) = \|12 \div 2 \div 3\| = \|2\| = 2$ (+ x - x - = +)	

Solve the following operations with integers: (answers on page 146)

1.) $31 + 72 =$

2.) $(-71) + (-89) =$

3.) $-21 - 8 =$

4.) $2 \times 2 \times (-7) =$

5.) $-3 \times 7 \times -3 =$

6.) $16 \div (-2) =$

7.) $-72 \div (-9) =$

Numbers and Mathematical Operations

Calculations with whole numbers, decimals, and fractions

Order of Operations (P.E.M.D.A.S – 'Please Excuse My Dear Aunt Sally'):

Parenthesis, Exponents, Multiplication, Division, Addition, Subtraction

Problem:	$7 + (6 * 5^2 + 3)$
Parenthesis	$7 + (6 * 5^2 + 3)$
Exponents	$7 + (6 * 25 + 3)$
Multiply	$7 + (150 + 3)$
Addition in parenthesis	$7 + (153)$
Addition	160

Practice Problems: (answers on page 147)

1.) $11 + 7(1 + 6)$ 2.) $19 - 3 + 2(1)$

3.) $30 + 2(50 \div 5 + 6)$ 4.) $7 + 8(1 + 6)$

You should be able to complete problems using order of operations skills. Also, the practice written response question is a math problem completed incorrectly. If you are out of practice with these types of problems, there are places online to practice.

Geometry
Procedures, tools, and units for problems

Procedure for Measuring: A proper measurement should always contain the measurement and the units of measure; for example; if the object is 12 by 12, are we talking about a patio or a sheet of paper? If the object is 12 feet by 12 feet, the unit is feet.

Proper Tools:

Measurement	Tools	Customary Unit	Metric Unit
Length	Ruler, yardstick, meter stick, tape measure	Inch, feet, yard, mile	Millimeter, centimeter, meter, kilometer
Perimeter	Ruler, yardstick, meter stick, tape measure	Inch, feet, yard, mile	Millimeter, centimeter, meter, kilometer
Area	Ruler, yardstick, meter stick, tape measure	Square inch, square feet, square yard, acre, square mile	**Square Units** millimeter, square centimeter, square meter, hectare, square kilometer
Weight	Scale	Ounce, pound, tons	Grams, kilograms, metric ton
Time	Clock, stop watch	Seconds, minutes, hours	Seconds, minutes, hours
Temperature	Thermometer	Fahrenheit	Celsius
Volume/Capacity	Measuring cups and spoons, beakers	Ounces, cups, pints, quarts, gallons, or cube units	**Cubed Units** Milliliters, liters

Geometry

Direct and indirect measurement using algebra or geometry

Direct Measurement – measures the exact item.

Indirect Measurement – measures something else to obtain a measurement; for example, measuring a tree's shadow to calculate its actual height. This is set up as a basic proportion.

Example: A tree is 18 feet tall and casts a shadow that measures 12 feet. Matt casts a shadow that measures 4 feet. How tall is Matt?

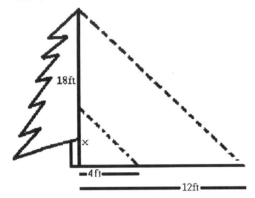

$$\frac{tree\ 18ft}{shadow\ 12ft} = \frac{Matt\ x}{shadow\ 4ft}$$

$$12x = 72$$

$$x = 6, so\ Matt\ is\ 6\ ft\ tall$$

These proportions can be used to solve the classic flag pole problem. If a tree is 8ft tall and cast a shadow that is 6ft and the flag pole cast a shadow of 24ft what is the height of the flag pole.

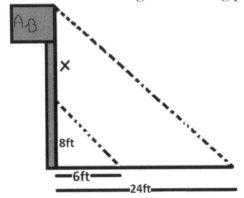

$$\frac{flag\ x}{tree\ 8ft} = \frac{shadow\ 24ft}{shadow\ 6ft}$$

$$192 = 6x$$

$$x = 32, so\ Flag\ pole\ is\ 32\ ft\ tall$$

Geometry

Classifying plane and solid geometric figures

Plane Figures – are flat figures, including, but not limited to, triangles, quadrilaterals, circles, rhombi, and squares. These are also known as two-dimensional shapes. These shapes have area, sides, and angles.
- Area – the amount of space occupied in a plane by a figure
- Side – the edge of a figure
- Angle – the union of two rays

Types of Plane Figures:
- Triangle – A 2-D shape with 3 straight sides and 3 angles. There are 6 types of triangles to consider. In terms of side length, there are the equilateral triangle with three equal sides, the isosceles triangle with two equal sides, and the scalene triangle with no equal sides. In terms of angle measurements, there are the acute triangle with all angles less than 90 degrees, the right triangle, which has one angle that measures 90 degrees, and the obtuse triangle, which has one angle that measures greater than 90 degrees.
- Quadrilaterals – A 2-D shape with 4 straight sides; examples are the rhombus and rectangle.
- Rectangles – A four-sided 2-D shape with 2 pairs of parallel sides that meet at right angles.
- Rhombi – A 2-D four-sided shape with opposite sides that are parallel and all sides are equal.
- Square – A 2-D shape with 4 sides of equal length and 4 right angles.
- Circle – A round, flat 2-D shape.

Solid Figures or Three-Dimensional Figures:
The defining difference between a 2-dimensional and a 3-dimensional shape is that a 3-D shape has volume or capacity.
Volume – the amount of space within an object.
Faces – a surface side of a shape; the cube, for example, has six faces.
Edge – the line where two faces meet.
Vertices – the place where three or more edges meet.

Geometry
Basic geometric concepts

Symmetry – occurs when one half of an object mirrors the other half.

Congruence – means that the shapes are of the same size, with corresponding angles and sides that have the same measurements.

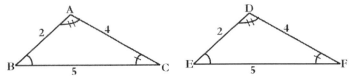

Similarity – is when two shapes are the same but have different sizes, and the corresponding angles are equal.

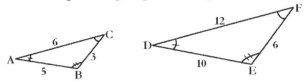

Transformations – describe a type of movement. There are three kinds: reflection, translation, and rotation.

Reflection	Translation	Rotation

Parallelism – Lines are parallel if they are always the same distance apart.

Perpendicular – means lines are at right angles to each other.

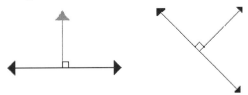

Geometry

Measuring components of geometric figures

Lines and Angles:
Line – is a set of points extending in opposite directions without an end. A line segment is a piece of line with no end points.

Ray – is a part of a line that begins at a point and continues without end in one direction.

Angle – is the opening that is formed when two lines, line segments, or rays intersect.

Vertex – is a point of an angle, polygon, or solid where two or more lines or line segments meet.

Angles:
An angle can be measured in degrees. The degrees can range from zero to 360°. A straight line or straight angle is 180°. An acute angle is 0° to 90°. A right angle is 90°. An obtuse angle is between 90° and 180°.

Right Angle, 90°	Straight Line, 180°	Acute Angle, 0° to 90°	Obtuse Angle, 90° to 180°

Complementary Angles – describes two angles that have a sum of 90°.

Supplementary Angles – describes two angles that have a sum of 180°.

Geometry

Measuring component of geometric figures

Vertical Angles – are formed when two lines intersect. Two of the resulting four angles are vertical angles, meaning they have the same measurement.

Adjacent Angles – are two angles that share a common side. These intersecting lines are supplementary, or have a sum of 180°.

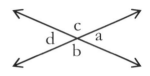

Vertical Angles
<d and <a, <c and <d

Adjacent Angles
<d and <c, <c and <a, <a and <b, <b and <d

Complete the following: (answers on page 147)

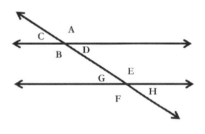

List Vertical Angles	List Adjacent Angles

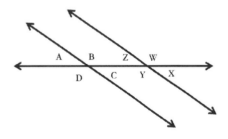

List Vertical Angles	List Adjacent Angles

Geometry
Measuring components of geometric figures

Perimeter – The distance around the outside edge of an object. The perimeter of a circle is called the circumference (C).
Common formulas or methods for *calculating perimeter:*

P = 2(l + w)   P = s + s + s   C = 2πr   P = 4(s)

Area – The measure of the entire surface of an object.
Common formulas or methods for *calculating area:*

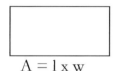

A = l x w   A = ½ bh   A = πr²   A = s²

Volume – The measure of the capacity of a figure.
Common formulas for or methods for *calculating volume:*

  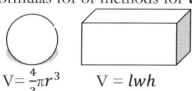

$V = s^3$ $V = \frac{4}{3}\pi r^3$ $V = lwh$ $V = \pi r^2 h$ $V = \frac{1}{3}bh$

Other - V of a cone $V = \frac{1}{3}\pi r^2 h$

Solve the Following: (answers on page 147-148)

1.) Find Perimeter and Area

2.) Find Circumference and Area

3.) Find Perimeter and Area

4.) Find Area

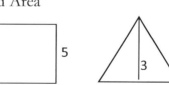

5.) Find Volume of the Sphere

6.) Find the Volume of the Cube

Geometry

Using the coordinate systems to identify basic geometric figures and concepts

Point – is a location in a plane or in space; it has no dimensions.
Line – is a set of points extending in opposite directions without an end.
Line Segment – is a piece of line with no end points.
Ray – is a line that extends in only one direction.
Angle – is the opening that is formed when two lines, line segments, or rays intersect.

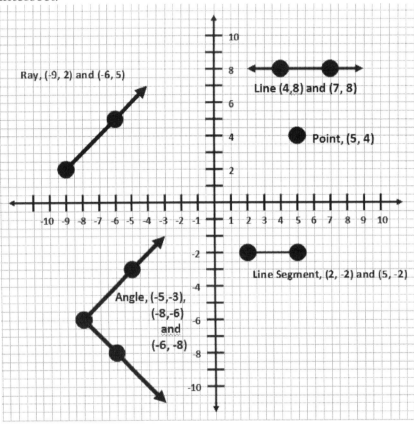

Algebra
Patterns

Patterns in Algebra — There are a number of patterns or sequences, which include growing patterns, number patterns, Fibonacci sequences, variable patterns, equations, and inequalities.

Growing Patterns:

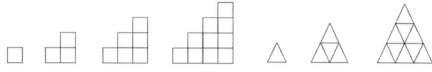

Arithmetic: 1, 6, 11, 16, 21, 26 (+5)
              1, 2, 6, 8, 10 (+2)

Geometric: 1, 4, 9, 16 (Squares $1^2, 2^2, 3^2, 4^2$)

Find the nest number in the sequence: (answers on page 149)
   1.) 1, 8, 27, 64…
   2.) 1, 3, 6, 10, 15…
   3.) 16, 19, 22, 25…
   4.) 23, 28, 33, 38…
   5.) Find the next figure:

   6.) Find the next figure:

Algebra

Variables, functions, and equations in the expression of algebraic relationships

Variable – is a letter or symbol that represents a number in an equation.

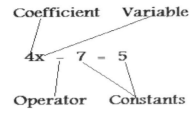

Algebraic Expressions:

Using the following, $x = 2, y = 4, z = 3$, to evaluate the algebraic expressions:

Example 1:	Example 2:	Example 3:
$7 + 3z$	$2xy^2 - 6$	$\dfrac{6 + 3x}{z}$
$7 + 9$ 16	$2(2)(4^2) - 6$ $2(2)(16) - 6$ $4(16) - 6$ $64 - 6$ 58	$\dfrac{6 + 3(2)}{3}$ $\dfrac{6 + 6}{3} = \dfrac{12}{3} = 4$

Real-world application of expressions:

It costs $3 per recorder for a music class, plus $20 to ship them. How much will it cost per 20, 40, 60, 80 recorders?

x	20	40	60	80
3x+20	3(20)+20 60+20 80	3(40)+20 120+20 140	3(60)+20 180+20 200	3(80)+20 240+20 260

Equations:

There are six groups of students and two teachers for a total of 26 people. How many students are in each group?

$$6n + 2 = 26$$
$$-2 = -2$$
$$\dfrac{6n}{6} = \dfrac{24}{6}$$
$$n = 4$$

There are four students in each group.

Algebra
Variables, functions, and equations in the expression of algebraic relationships

Functions in Algebra:
A function is the study of how one variable will create change in another variable. It is a rule for a given situation of how the first variable will affect the second. Functions are often represented with f(x).

Example: The drama club is selling cookies after lunch to raise money for a field trip. They sell each cookie for $.50. It costs $.20 per cookie; therefore, their profit is $.30 per cookie. The club also spent $15.00 advertising the upcoming cookie sale.

To calculate their profit, we can use a function because the profit depends on the total number of cookies sold. So, a cookie sold is represented with "c," and we can calculate this with the following equation:

$(\textbf{cost per cookie x total cookies sold})-$
$(\textbf{cost to make each cookie x total cookies sold})-$
$\textbf{advertising} =$
$\textbf{profit} \text{ or } (.\textbf{50 x c})-(.\textbf{20 x c}) - \textbf{15} = \textbf{profit}$

Or, to simplify the calculation:
$(\textbf{profit per cookie x number sold})-\$\textbf{15} = \textbf{profit},$ or
$(.\textbf{30 x c}) - \textbf{15} = \textbf{profit},$ or written as a function, $30c - 15 = y$, or
$.\textbf{30}c - \textbf{15} = f(x)$

10 Cookies Sold	100 Cookies Sold	500 Cookies Sold
$.30(10) - 15 = y$	$.30(100) - 15 = y$	$.30(500) - 15 = y$
$3 - 15 = -10$	$30 - 15 = 15$	$150 - 15 = 135$

Algebra
Variables, functions, and equations in the expression of algebraic relationships

Four Basic Operations with Variables:

Ex.
$$20 + x = 27$$
$$-20 \quad -20$$
$$x = 7$$

Ex.
$$x - 17 = 5$$
$$+17 \quad +17$$
$$x = 22$$

Ex.
$$5x = 25$$
$$\frac{5x}{5} \quad \frac{25}{5}$$
$$x = 5$$

Ex.
$$\frac{x}{10} = 5$$

$$\frac{x}{10} = 5 \rightarrow$$
mult both sides by 10 then reduce. So ...
$$\frac{10x}{10} = 5 \times 10$$
$$x = 50$$

Solve the following: (answers on page 149)

1.) $55 + x = 87$

2.) $x - 19 = 7$

3.) $7x = 28$

4.) $\frac{x}{20} = 4$

Algebra

Relationships among variables based on mathematical expressions, tables, and graphs

Table – a way to organize information.

Total Number of Teachers Per Grade	
Grade	Teachers
K	12
1	9
2	11
3	9
4	8
5	10

*Note: There is one teacher for every 25 students.

Bar Graph: **Line Graph:**

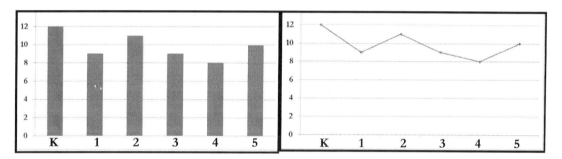

Expression – This is a combination of operations that contain letters (variables) and numbers. Example: $25x$, which means $25 \cdot x$

Equation – This is an algebraic expression that has an equal sign (=). In the data example, there are 25 students per teacher, so to figure out how many students are in each grade, use $25(t) = s$, where "t" is the number of teachers and "s" is the total number of students. An equation is $expression = expression$.

Verbal Description – Data can be represented in a total verbal form. For the above data, in the school there are a total of 59 teachers. For each teacher, there are 25 students.

Algebra
Solving equations and inequalities

Linear Equations – are equations that have a single variable.

One Step:

$$
\begin{array}{c|c|c|c}
x + 2 = 5 & x + 7 = -2 & -9x = -45 & 6x = 54 \\
-2\ -2 & -7\ \ -7 & \overline{-9\quad\ -9} & \overline{6\quad\ 6} \\
\hline
x\ \ = 3 & x\ \ = -9 & x = 5 & x = 9
\end{array}
$$

Two Step:

$$3x + 4 = 16$$
$$\underline{-4\ -4\ \ \ \ \ }$$
$$\frac{3x}{3} = \frac{12}{3}$$
$$x = 4$$

$$\frac{x}{3} = -14 + 9$$
$$\frac{x}{3} = -5$$
$$(3)\frac{x}{3} = -5(3)$$
$$x = -15$$

Solve the following: (answers on page 149-150)

1.) $7x + 8 = 92$

2.) $2x + 2 = 6$

3.) $x + 4 - 2x = -4$

4.) $7x + 2 = 2x - 3$

5.) $2(4 + 5x) = 58$

Algebra
Solving equations and inequalities

Inequalities:

Symbol	Words	Example
<	Less than	7 + x < 12
>	Greater than	12 – x > 7
≥	Greater than or equal to	3x ≥ 21
≤	Less than or equal to	2x + 6 ≤ 8

To solve inequalities using addition, subtraction, multiplication, and division, utilize methods used for solving any other equation. The inequality sign simply takes the place of the "=" sign.

These are equations that have more than one answer. The answer is generally placed on a graph to show the possible answers. ○ is used to depict < or > on a number line. ● is used to depict ≤ or ≥ on a number line.

$$x - 7 < -3$$
$$+7 \quad +7$$
$$x < 4$$

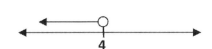

$$-3x - 3 =< 6$$
$$+3 \quad +3$$
$$\frac{-3x}{-3} \quad \frac{< 9}{-3}$$
$$x > 3$$

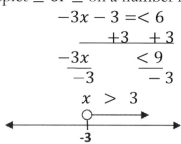

NOTE!!!! If you multiply or divide by a negative number, you have to reverse the inequality symbol.

$$x + 4 > 3$$
$$-4 \quad -4$$
$$x > -1$$

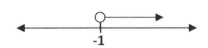

$$5 - x < 3$$
$$-5 \quad -5$$
$$\frac{-x}{-1} \quad \frac{< -2}{-1}$$
$$x > 2$$

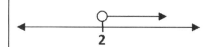

Note: Whenever you divide by a negative, you always reverse the inequality sign.

133

Algebra
One- and two-step linear equations and inequalities

$$4x + 6 \leq 3x - 5$$
$$ -6 -6$$
$$4x \leq 3x - 11$$
$$-3x -3x$$
$$x \leq -11$$

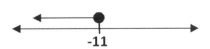

$$\frac{-2x}{-2} > \frac{4}{-2}$$
$$x < -2$$

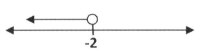

Note: Whenever you divide by a negative, you always reverse the inequality sign.

Solve the following: (answers on pages 150)

1.) $21 + x < 37$

2.) $2.25 - x > 1.2$

3.) $7x \leq 196$

4.) $\dfrac{x}{9} \geq 28$

5.) $15x - 3 > 132$

6.) $\dfrac{x}{7} - 1 > 2$

7.) $13 + x < 22$

Algebra
Algebraic functions to plot points, describe graphs, and determine slope

Ordered Pair – a pair of numbers that have a place on a coordinate plane, (x, y). The "x-axis" is the horizontal axis, and the "y-axis" is the vertical axis.

Coordinate Plane – has an x-axis and a y-axis, and there are four quadrants, numbered I, II, III, IV. The first quadrant is the upper right, and both the x and y are positive. The second quadrant is the upper left, and the x is negative and the y is positive. The third quadrant is the lower left, and both the x and y are negative. The fourth quadrant is the lower right, and the x is positive and the y is negative.

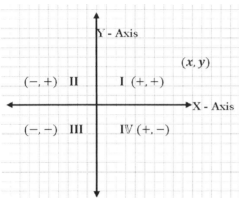

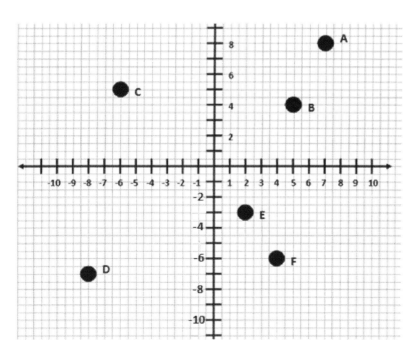

Name the following points and graph the ordered pairs:

Plot the following: (answers on page 151)

1.) (3, 5)

2.) (-4, -2)

3.) (-3, 8)

4.) (8, -4)

List the ordered pairs for the following points: (answers on page 151)
A) (7, 8)   B)   C)   D)

E)   F)

135

Algebra

Algebraic functions to plot points, describe graphs, and determine slope

Slope:
Graphing in Algebra – In elementary school, students are introduced to graphing, and the equation of a line is $y = mx + b$.

Determining Slope – Slope shows how steep a straight line is. To calculate slope use the following:

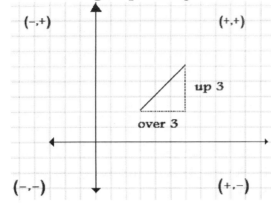

Slope is denoted with the letter m.

$$Slope = \frac{rise}{run}$$

$$Slope = \frac{3}{3} \text{ or } 1$$

Slope can also be calculated using an equation, when you have at least two ordered pairs from the line.

$$m = \frac{change\ in\ y}{change\ in\ x} \text{ or } \frac{y_2 - y_1}{x_2 - x_1}$$

Using the illustration, we find the ordered pairs (3, 2) and (6, 5).

$$\frac{y_2 - y_1}{x_2 - x_1} \rightarrow \frac{5_2 - 2_1}{6_2 - 3_1} = \frac{3}{3} = 1$$

You can also find the slope intercept using the following equation:
$y = mx + b$, where y = y in the ordered pair, m = the slope, x = x in the ordered pair, and b = the intersecting numbers.

When given the ordered pair (2, 6) with a slope of 2,

$$y = mx + b$$

$$6 = 2(2) + b$$

$$6 = 4 + b$$

$$2 = b$$

Algebra

Algebra represents relationships and patterns in everyday life

The most classic example of patterns is the Fibonacci Sequence: 0, 1, 1, 2, 3, 5, 8, 13, where the sum of the previous two numbers in the sequence equals the third. There are many representations of this sequence found in nature. Using your favorite search engine, search the phrase "Fibonacci Sequence in Nature." I think you will be amazed at how often this pattern is repeated throughout our world.

Data Analysis

Methods for organizing and interpreting data in a variety of formats and analyzing data

Data Tables – When getting ready for an experiment, you need to have a way to record your data. To communicate the information gathered during an experiment, you must choose the appropriate graph or table to show the results. Tables and graphs often give great visuals for data gathered.

Bar Graphs – are used to organize and display data for different categories.
   Steps to create a bar graph:
   1) Start by graphing a horizontal and vertical axis.
   2) Write category names along the horizontal axis.
   3) Label the vertical axis with the corresponding variables.
   4) Draw a solid bar using the vertical axis.
   5) Add a title that describes the graph.

Line Graphs – are used to display data that shows how one variable (responding variable) changes in response to the other variable (manipulated variable).
   Steps to create a line graph:
   1) Start by drawing a horizontal and vertical axis.
   2) Label the horizontal axis with manipulated variables. Label the vertical axis with responding variables, being sure to include units of measure.
   3) Create a scale or range of the data collected, ensuring that the numbers are evenly spaced.
   4) Plot the points on the graph.
   5) Connect the plotted points.
   6) Title the axis for each.

Data Analysis

Methods for organizing and interpreting data in a variety of formats and analyzing data

Bar Graph – an arrangement of info or data into columns and rows or a condensed list.

Example: Sports children like to watch or play:

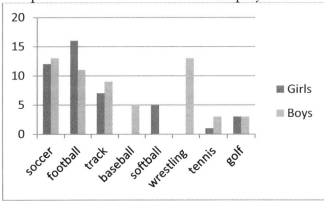

Answer the following questions using the above bar graph: (answers on page 151)
   1.) How many total children like to watch or play soccer?
   2.) Estimate how many children participated in the survey?

Frequency Distribution – a table that lists a set of scores and their frequency (how many times each item occurs).

List of test scores: 100, 100, 80, 80, 80, 80, 80, 70, 70, 70, 70, 60, 60, 50.

Scores	Frequency
100	2
80	5
70	4
60	2
50	1

Answer the following questions using the above frequency table: (answers on page 151)
   1.) Which grade was most common on the test?
   2.) Which grade was the least common on the test?

Data Analysis

Methods for organizing and interpreting data in a variety of formats and analyzing data

Picture Graph – is a visual representation of data. A picture is used to represent a certain quantity of data.

Favorite Classroom Snack*	
Cookies	◯◯◯◯◯◯
Ice Cream	🍦🍦
Chips	◯◯◯
Fruit	◯◯◯
Cake	🍰🍰🍰🍰
Vegetables	🥕

*1 picture = 2 students

Answer the following questions using the above picture graph: (answers on page 151)
1.) How many students like chips as their favorite classroom snack?
2.) Each picture represents how many students?

Line Graph – a graph that uses points connected by a line to show trends.
Favorite Classroom Snack

Answer the following questions using the above line graph: (answers on page 152)
1.) Which snack is the least popular?
2.) Which snack is the most popular?

139

Data Analysis

Methods for organizing and interpreting data in a variety of formats and analyzing data

Circle Graphs (aka pie chart) – circular chart divided into sectors; these sectors total 100%.

Favorite Classroom Snack

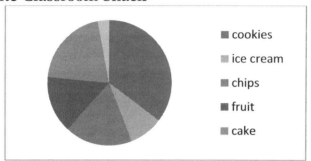

Answer the following questions using the above circle graph: (answers on page 152)
    1.) Estimate the percentage of students who like chips and ice cream.
    2.) What does the chart show?

Data Analysis
Standard measures used to describe data

Mean or Average – To find the mean or average of a group of numbers, add all numbers together, then divide the sum by how many numbers there are.

    A student has three grades: 80, 75, and 90.
    Add these numbers together: $80 + 75 + 90 = 245$

There are three grades; so we divide the total by three. The result is the average/mean $\frac{245}{3} = 81.6$

Median – This is literally the middle number in a sorted/ordered list.

Example:
List: 5, 10, 6, 7, 12
First put the numbers in order: 5, 6, 7, 10, 12. The middle number is 7, so it is the median. If there are two middle numbers, find the average or mean of the numbers and that is the median.

Mode – This is the number in a set that occurs **m**ost **o**ften.

Range – This is the difference between the lowest and the highest values. For the set {67, 69, 75, 80, 81, 82, 90}, the range is calculated as 90-67=23.

Practice finding mean, median, mode, and range with the following sets of numbers: (answers on page 152)

    1.) 5, 5, 7, 11, 15
    2.) 3, 12, 11, 15, 14, 15
    3.) 50, 50, 55, 55, 55, 70, 80, 85

Answers and Solution for Math Review

Page 97

1.) -5 2.) $7 + 27$ 3.) $\dfrac{x}{4}$

Page 99

1.) $<$ 2.) $>$ 3.) $<$

Page 100

1.) $>$ 2.) $>$ 3.) $>$

Page 102

1.) $\dfrac{1}{3}, \dfrac{1}{2}, \dfrac{5}{7}, \dfrac{4}{5}$

2.) $0.002, 0.02, 0.2, 1.02$

3.) $0, 0.25\%, 0.11, 70\%$

Page 103

1.) 273.5   2.) 1.6   3.) 57.1   4.) 5,400
5.) 200   6.) 11,700   7.) 4,200

Page 105

1.) 24   1, 2, 3, 4, 6, 8, 12, 24
    36   1, 2, 3, 4, 6, 9, 12, 18, 36

2.) 18   1, 2, 3, 6, 18
    36   1, 2, 3, 4, 6, 9, 12, 18, 36
    42   1, 2, 3, 6, 7, 14, 21, 42

3.) 12   1, 2, 3, 4, 6, 12
    56   1, 2, 4, 7, 8, 14, 28, 56
    60   1, 2, 3, 4, 5, 6, 10, 12, 15, 20, 30, 60

4.) 9   1, 3, 9
    63   1, 3, 7, 9, 21, 63

Answers and Solution for Math Review

Page 106

1.) 12

$$\frac{20\%}{100} = \frac{x}{60} \rightarrow 20 \times 60 = 100 \times X \rightarrow 1200 = 100x$$
$$\rightarrow \frac{1200}{100} = \frac{100x}{100} \rightarrow 12 = x \rightarrow so\ 12\ is\ 20\%\ of\ 60$$

2.) 2

$$\frac{10\%}{100} = \frac{.2}{x} \rightarrow 10 \times x = 100 \times .2 \rightarrow 10x = 20$$
$$\rightarrow \frac{10x}{10} = \frac{20}{10} \rightarrow 2 = x \rightarrow so\ .2\ is\ 10\%\ of\ 2$$

3.) 2

$$\frac{x\%}{100} = \frac{6}{300} \rightarrow x \times 300 = 100 \times 6 \rightarrow 300x = 600$$
$$\rightarrow \frac{300x}{300} = \frac{600}{300} \rightarrow 2 = x \rightarrow so\ 6\ is\ 2\%\ of\ 300$$

4.) 2.56

$$\frac{4.8\%}{100} = \frac{x}{32} \rightarrow 8 \times 32 = 100 \times X \rightarrow 1536 = 100x$$
$$\rightarrow \frac{1536}{100} = \frac{100x}{100} \rightarrow 2.56 = x \rightarrow so\ 15.36\ is\ 8\%\ of\ 32$$

Page 107

1.) $\frac{1}{4}$

$$\frac{0.25}{1} = \frac{0.25}{1} \times \frac{100}{100} = \frac{25}{100} = \frac{1}{4}$$

2.) $\frac{4}{5}$

$$\frac{0.80}{1} = \frac{0.80}{1} \times \frac{100}{100} = \frac{80}{100} = \frac{8}{10} = \frac{4}{5}$$

3.) $\frac{13}{20}$

$$\frac{0.65}{1} = \frac{0.65}{1} \times \frac{100}{100} = \frac{65}{100} = \frac{13}{20}$$

Answers and Solution for Math Review

Page 107

1.) .333 repeating

```
   .33
 3)100
  -3
   10
   -9
    1
```

2.) .833 repeating

```
   .83
 6)500
  -48
   20
  -18
   20
```

Page 108

1.) $25\% = \dfrac{25}{100} = \dfrac{1}{4}$

2.) $45\% = \dfrac{45}{100} = \dfrac{9}{20}$

3.) $30\% = \dfrac{30}{100} = \dfrac{3}{10}$

Page 108

1.) $\dfrac{1}{2} = \dfrac{1}{2} \times \dfrac{x}{100} = 1 \times 100$ and $2x \rightarrow 2x = 100 \rightarrow x = 50 \rightarrow \dfrac{50}{100} \rightarrow$ **50%**

2.) $\dfrac{2}{3} = \dfrac{2}{3} \times \dfrac{x}{100} = 2 \times 100$ and $3x \rightarrow 3x = 200 \rightarrow x = 66 \rightarrow \dfrac{66}{100} \rightarrow$ **66.667%**

3.) $\dfrac{4}{5} = \dfrac{4}{5} \times \dfrac{x}{100} = 4 \times 100$ and $5x \rightarrow 5x = 400 \rightarrow x = 80 \rightarrow \dfrac{80}{100} \rightarrow$ **80%**

Page 109

1.) 450%   2.) 25.9%   3.) 4560%

Page 109

1.) .22   2.) .07   3.) .196

Answers and Solution for Math Review

Page 113

1.) $\dfrac{2}{3} \div \dfrac{5}{6}$
$= \dfrac{2}{3} \times \dfrac{6}{5}$
$= \dfrac{12}{15} \text{ or } \dfrac{4}{5}$

2.) $-\dfrac{1}{7} \times \dfrac{7}{10}$
$= -\dfrac{7}{70} \text{ or }$
$-\dfrac{1}{10}$

3.) $\dfrac{2}{3} + \dfrac{5}{9}$
$= \dfrac{2(3)}{3(3)} + \dfrac{5}{9}$
$= \dfrac{6}{9} + \dfrac{5}{9}$
$= \dfrac{11}{9} \text{ or } 1\dfrac{2}{9}$

4.) $\dfrac{7}{8} \div 6 = \dfrac{7}{8} \times \dfrac{1}{6}$
$= \dfrac{7}{48}$

5.) $\dfrac{2}{3} \times \dfrac{7}{8}$
$= \dfrac{14}{24} \text{ or } \dfrac{7}{12}$

6.) $\dfrac{9}{10} - 5$
$= \dfrac{9}{10} - \dfrac{5}{1}$
$= \dfrac{9}{10} - \dfrac{5(10)}{1(10)}$
$= \dfrac{9}{10} - \dfrac{50}{10}$
$= -\dfrac{41}{10} \text{ or }$
$-4\dfrac{1}{10}$

7.) $\dfrac{5}{12} - \dfrac{1}{9}$
$= \dfrac{5(3)}{12(3)} - \dfrac{1(4)}{9(4)}$
$= \dfrac{15}{36} - \dfrac{4}{36} = \dfrac{11}{36}$

8.) $\dfrac{7}{8} + \dfrac{1}{20}$
$= \dfrac{7(5)}{8(5)} + \dfrac{1(2)}{20(2)}$
$= \dfrac{35}{40} + \dfrac{2}{40} = \dfrac{37}{40}$

Answers and Solution for Math Review

Page 114

1.) Identify the base and the exponent in the following 5^3.

5^3

base 5,
exponent 3

2.) What is 3^4?

3^4
$3 \times 3 \times 3 \times 3$
$9 \times 3 \times 3$
27×3
81

3.) What is 4^5?

4^5
$4 \times 4 \times 4 \times 4 \times 4$
$16 \times 4 \times 4 \times 4$
64×16
1024

4.) What is 3^{-4}?

3^{-4}
$\dfrac{1}{3 \times 3 \times 3 \times 3}$
$\dfrac{1}{9 \times 3 \times 3}$
$\dfrac{1}{27 \times 3}$
$\dfrac{1}{81}$

5.) What is 2^{-3}?

2^{-3}
$\dfrac{1}{2 \times 2 \times 2}$
$\dfrac{1}{4 \times 2}$
$\dfrac{1}{8}$

6.) $(\dfrac{1}{2})^3$

$(\dfrac{1}{2})^3$
$\dfrac{1}{2} \times \dfrac{1}{2} \times \dfrac{1}{2}$
$\dfrac{1}{4} \times \dfrac{1}{2}$
$\dfrac{1}{8}$

Page 115

1.) 33.55	2.) 2.66	3.) 8.452
4.) 241.65	5.) 1.8	6.) 60.2583

Page 117

1.) 103	2.) -160	3.) -29	4.) -28
5.) 63	6.) -8	7.) 8	

Answers and Solution for Math Review

Page 118

1.) 11+7(1+6)	2.) 19−3+2(1)	3.) 30+2(50÷5+6)	4.) 7+8(1+6)
11+7(7)	19−3+2	30+2(10+6)	7+8(7)
11+49	16+2	30+2(16)	7+56
60	**18**	30+32	**63**
	*note, we add and subtract from left to right when there are no other symbols present	**62**	

Page 124

1.)   List Vertical Angles   List Adjacent Angles

∠A & ∠B   ∠C & ∠G   ∠A & ∠C   ∠C & ∠F
∠A & ∠E   ∠C & ∠H   ∠A & ∠D   ∠D & ∠E
∠A & ∠F   ∠D & ∠G   ∠A & ∠H   ∠E & ∠G
∠B & ∠E   ∠D & ∠H   ∠B & ∠C   ∠E & ∠H
∠B & ∠F   ∠E & ∠F   ∠B & ∠D   ∠F & ∠H
∠C & ∠D   ∠G & ∠H   ∠B & ∠G   ∠F & ∠G

2.)   List Vertical Angles   List Adjacent Angles

∠A & ∠C   ∠C & ∠Z   ∠A & ∠B   ∠B & ∠Z
∠A & ∠X   ∠D & ∠B   ∠A & ∠D   ∠C & ∠D
∠A & ∠Z   ∠D & ∠W   ∠A & ∠W   ∠C & ∠W
∠B & ∠W   ∠D & ∠Y   ∠A & ∠Y   ∠C & ∠Y
∠B & ∠Y   ∠W & ∠Y   ∠B & ∠C   ∠Y & ∠X
∠C & ∠X   ∠Z & ∠X   ∠B & ∠X   ∠Z & ∠W

Page 125

1.) Find Perimeter and Area:

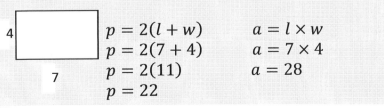

$p = 2(l + w)$ $a = l \times w$
$p = 2(7 + 4)$ $a = 7 \times 4$
$p = 2(11)$ $a = 28$
$p = 22$

Answers and Solution for Math Review

Page 125 cont.

2.) Find circumference and Area:

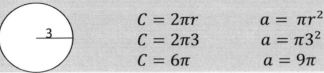

$C = 2\pi r$ $a = \pi r^2$
$C = 2\pi 3$ $a = \pi 3^2$
$C = 6\pi$ $a = 9\pi$

3.) Find Perimeter and Area:

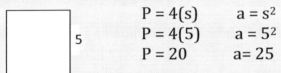

P = 4(s)   a = s²
P = 4(5)   a = 5²
P = 20   a = 25

4.) Find Area:

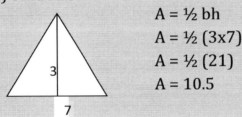

A = ½ bh
A = ½ (3x7)
A = ½ (21)
A = 10.5

5.) $V = \frac{4}{3}\pi r^3$

$V = \frac{4}{3}\pi 2^3$

$V = \frac{4}{3}\pi (2 \times 2 \times 2)$

$V = \frac{4}{3}\pi (8)$

$V = 33.5 units^3$

6.) $V = s^3$

$V = 4^3$

$V = (4 \times 4 \times 4)$

$V = (12 \times 4)$

$V = 48 units^3$

Answers and Solution for Math Review

Page 127

1.) 125
2.) 21
3.) 28
4.) 43
5.)
6.)

Page 130

1.)
$$55 + x = 87$$
$$-55 \quad -55$$
$$x = 35$$

2.)
$$x - 19 = 7$$
$$+19 + 19$$
$$x = 26$$

3.)
$$\frac{7x}{7} = \frac{28}{7}$$
$$x = 4$$

4.)
$$\frac{x}{20} = 4 \rightarrow \frac{20x}{20} = 4 \times 20$$
$$x = 80$$

Page 132

1.) $7x + 8 = 92$
$$7x + 8 = 92$$
$$-8 \quad -8$$
$$\frac{7x}{7} = \frac{84}{7}$$
$$x = 12$$

2.) $2x + 2 = 6$
$$2x + 2 = 6$$
$$-2 \quad -2$$
$$\frac{2x}{2} = \frac{4}{2}$$
$$x = 2$$

3.) $x + 4 - 2x = -4$
$$x + 4 - 2x = -4$$
$$-4 \quad\quad -4$$
$$x - 2x = -8$$
$$\frac{-1x}{-1} = \frac{-8}{-1}$$
$$x = 8$$

4.) $7x + 2 = 2x - 3$
$$7x + 2 = 2x - 3$$
$$-2 \quad\quad -2$$
$$7x = 2x - 5$$
$$-2x - 2x$$
$$\frac{5x}{5} = \frac{-5}{5}$$
$$x = -1$$

Answers and Solution for Math Review

Page 132

5.) $2(4 + 5x) = 58$

$$2(4 + 5x) = 58$$
$$8 + 10x = 58$$
$$\underline{-8 \qquad\quad -8}$$
$$10x = 50$$
$$\overline{10} \quad\; \overline{10}$$
$$x = 5$$

Page 134

1.)
$$21 + x < 37$$
$$\underline{-21 \qquad -21}$$
$$x < 16$$

2.)
$$2.25 - x > 1.2$$
$$\underline{-2.25 \qquad -2.25}$$
$$\underline{-x > -1.05}$$
$$-1 \quad\; -1$$
$$\mathbf{x < 1.05}$$

*remember when you ÷ by a negative you 'flip' the inequality sign

3.)
$$\underline{7x \leq 196}$$
$$7 \qquad 7$$
$$\mathbf{x \leq 28}$$

4.)
$$\frac{x}{9} \geq 28 \rightarrow \frac{9x}{9} \geq 9 \times 28$$
$$\mathbf{x \geq 252}$$

5.)
$$15x - 3 > 132$$
$$\underline{+3 \quad\; +3}$$
$$\underline{15x > 135}$$
$$15 \qquad 15$$
$$\mathbf{x > 9}$$

6.)
$$\frac{x}{7} - 1 > 2 \rightarrow \frac{x}{7} > 3 \rightarrow$$
$$\frac{7x}{7} > 7 \times 3$$
$$\mathbf{x > 21}$$

7.)
$$13 + x < 22$$
$$\underline{-13 \qquad -13}$$
$$\mathbf{x < 9}$$

Answers and Solution for Math Review

Page 135

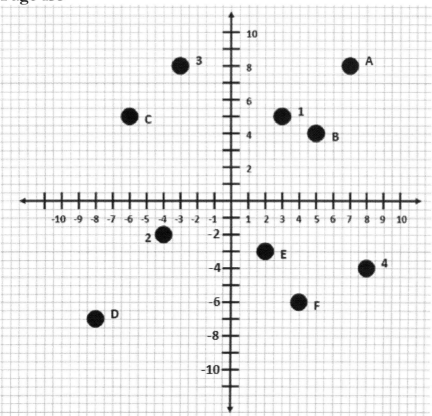

A) (7, 8)   B) (5, 4)   C) (-6, 5)   D) (-8, -7)
E) (2, -3)   F) (4, -6)

Page 138
1.) $12 + 13 = 25$
2.) 100 students

Page 138
1.) 80
2.) 50

Page 139
1.) 6 students
2.) 2 students

Answers and Solution for Math Review

Page 139
1.) Vegetables
2.) Cookies

Page 140
1.) 25%
2.) The favorite classroom snack

Page 141
1.) 5, 5, 7, 11, 15
   Mean: 8.6
   Median: 7
   Mode: 5
   Range: 10

2.) 3, 11, 12, 14, 15, 15
   Mean: 11.66
   Median: 11
   Mode: 15
   Range: 12

3.) 50, 50, 55, 55, 55, 70, 80, 85
   Mean: 62.5
   Median: 55
   Mode: 55
   Range: 35

Science

This section is organized according to the frameworks available in PDF format from the GACE website, www.gace.nesinc.com. There are four objectives for this section: characteristics of science, earth science, physical science, and life science.

Items in this section:
- ☑ Characteristics and processes of science
- ☑ Earth science
- ☑ Physical science
- ☑ Life science

Characteristics and Processes of Science
Nature of scientific knowledge

Purpose of:
- Curiosity – drives scientific inquiry; imagine the world if scientists had not been curious about the world we live in.
- Honesty – This means that we report our findings truthfully; scientists have to be honest, especially with the results of experiments.
- Openness, or Open-Mindedness – Scientists have to be capable of accepting new and different ideas.
- Skepticism – Scientists have to be skeptical of evidence that has no data to back it up.
- Reliance of Verifiable Evidence – Scientists have to test other theories. The more times a scientist comes up with the same results, the more valid the theory becomes.

Characteristics and Processes of Science
Scientific inquiry and the design of scientific investigations

Steps of Scientific Inquiry:
- **Pose a Question** – Scientific inquiry begins with a question, usually after an observation is made; for example, "What factors can increase the growth rate of a pea plant?"
- **Develop a Hypothesis** – A hypothesis is a possible explanation to a set of observations and must be testable; for example, "Blue light will make a pea plant grow faster than clear light."
- **Design an Experiment** – An experiment must be a controlled experiment, with a manipulated variable and a responding variable.
    - Control Variable – is the factor that does not change.
    - Manipulated Variable – is the factor that the scientist changes.
    - Responding Variable – is the result of the manipulated variable.
- **Collect and Interpret Data** – As the experiment is carried out, data is collected and organized into charts and graphs, which are interpreted.
- **Draw Conclusions** – Make a decision on what you interpret from your experiment.
- **Communicate** – Share your results with the scientific community.

Characteristics and Processes of Science

Unifying concepts of science

The unifying concepts of science as outlined by the National Science Standards, courtesy of www.nap.edu, are:

- **Systems, Order, and Organization** – This concept explains that everything in science is part of an organized, ordered system.
- **Evidence, Models, and Explanation** – This concept explains that we use evidence and models to explain the world around us.
- **Change, Constancy, and Measurement** – This concept explains the fact that measurement is important for consistency of data. This allows any changing idea to be accurately documented.
- **Evolution and Equilibrium** – This concept explains that everything in science follows an evolutionary path. This means that the hypothesis progresses through the steps of the scientific process. It is also important to understand that everything in science is part of nature's balancing act, that each thing affects the other thing.
- **Form and Function** – This concept explains the fact that science follows form/rules and that science, itself, outlines the rules and laws. There is also nothing in science that does/did not have a function.
- **System** – is a group of parts that work as a whole. Example: Earth science – The earth's four spheres work together to form the earth's system. Life science – The human body is made up of organ systems.
- **Characteristics of Systems** –
  - Systems have organized structure.
  - Systems are arranged in a hierarchy.
  - Systems consist of interrelated components.
  - Systems have inputs and outputs.
- **Characteristics of Models** – help to explain things that are complex or cannot be observed directly, such as a model of DNA, cells, the universe, or atoms. Also, computer-generated models are used to predict the weather. Models can also demonstrate changes. They are used to predict the effects of ocean height on shorelines.
- **Advantages** – Give individuals the option to view three-dimensional representations of ideas and concepts. Models make it possible to view the entire solar system and to see the detail of an atom. They are used to replicate intricate systems which are hard to study.
- **Disadvantages** – Have to interpret scale and some detail must be left off for large applications.
- **Limitations** – may not be to scale or exact.

Characteristics and Processes of Science
Strategies for observing, collecting, analyzing, and communicating scientific data

Observing and Collecting – is when one uses their five senses to gather information. Observations must be an accurate report of what one's senses detect. With an observation, one does not manipulate or assist the subject. Also, the subject is usually observed in its natural habitat. Examples of observation are the moon phases and types of vegetation in an area. It is important that students know what they are 'looking' for. Having a classroom set of clipboards is a good way to get students in observation and collection mode. Ask them to write down what they see. It is important to practice this before students complete an experiment.

Analyzing and Communicating Scientific Data – These steps are all about organizing data and presenting the information that is collected. During these steps it is important to have students decide what information is important to the scientific problem.

After the information is displayed, ask yourself: Does it support your hypothesis? Does it point to a flaw in the experiment? Do you need more data?

Explaining and Communicating Investigations, Data, Evidence, and Results – Once you have gathered and organized your data, you may see an immediate trend or the need to collect more data. The results of the experiment may lead to more problems to be solved.

Data is one of the most important components of scientific investigation. Data allows scientific peers to communicate and replicate the investigation.

Scientists communicate their findings through a variety of mediums. Journals are most common. Scientists write articles with the details of their experiment and their findings. The articles are published for the scientific community. The scientist's peers will review and respond to the published findings. Most journals are available via the Internet. Scientists also attend meetings to share their findings on similar topics in similar fields.

Characteristics and Processes of Science

Appropriate tools, skills, and safety associated with scientific investigations

Choosing the Appropriate Tools and Instruments of Science to Gather Data:

- **Mass** – is the amount of matter in an object. This is measured in grams (g) and kilograms (kg) using a balance.
- **Liquid Volume** – is the amount of space the liquid takes up. This is measured in liters (l) and milliliters (ML) using graduated cylinders.
- **Length** – is the distance between two points. This is measured in meters (m), kilometers (km), and centimeters (cm) using metric rulers and meter sticks.
- **Temperature** – is the measure of how hot or cold a substance is. This is measured in degrees Celsius (°C) using a Celsius thermometer. Note that water freezes at 0°C.
- **Time** – is measured in seconds.
- **Area** – is the measure of the surface or portion covered by an object. It is measured in square units. Area is measured in meters (m^2), kilometers (km^2), and centimeters (cm^2) using metric rulers and meter sticks.

In grades K-5 there are many opportunities for scientific experimentations and lab activities. It is important to educate students about the tools they will encounter. Also, this is when it is time for students to learn about proper safety and the methods and processes used in science.

Common Tools – rulers, scales, beakers, cylinders, and the five senses.

Process Skills:
- Observing – using your five senses.
- Inferring – when you explain or interpret the things you observe.
- Predicting – means making a forecast of what will happen in the future based on past experience or evidence.

Safety Procedures:
This is an important part of setting up a lab for students. In most cases the lab is going to be predesigned for you and there will be an attached materials list. However, you know your students, so it is up to you to decide what materials are appropriate for their use. You need to keep allergies, fears, and culture conflicts in mind when planning lab activities.

Characteristics and Processes of Science

Appropriate tools, skills, and safety associated with scientific investigations

General Safety:
Introduce the lab activity to students and be sure to reiterate all safety rules, highlighting the ones that specifically relate to the lab or activity the students are about to complete. Remind students that horseplay is unacceptable and that no eating or drinking is allowed.

Glassware Safety:
- When glassware is broken or chipped, discard it in the proper manner.
- The teacher should always place glass tubes or thermometers into rubber stoppers.

Sharp Instruments:
- Handle sharp tools/instruments with extreme care.
- Do not cut toward yourself.

Heating and Fire Safety:
- Keep combustible material away from fire.
- When heating a test tube, ensure that the opening is pointing away.
- Never heat a substance in a closed container.
- Always use an oven mitt.

Chemical Safety:
- Never touch, taste, or smell chemicals.
- Never put your face near the opening of a container.
- Use only chemicals needed for the activity.
- Keep chemical containers closed.

Plants and animals are a fascinating addition to the classroom, but it is important to educate students on their proper care and handling.

Never experiment with animals. Only handle plants and animals when needed. It is very important to know if students have allergies to animal hair or dander. Also, be informed of any plant allergies. Wash hands after handling plants and animals.

Characteristics and Processes of Science

Connections among science, mathematics, technology, society, and everyday life

Science is everywhere and embedded within our lives; it is important that students know this. If you have not been in the classroom yet, you will soon understand how vital it is to make content connections as well as real life connections. It is important that students know and 'see' why they are learning information before they get to the point of frustration and ask, "Why do I need to know this?" We use math in science daily to make calculations and understand and interpret data. Science has improved through technological advances. Science has and can change society; for example, through science and math, the Romans figured out how to bring water to the city in aqueducts. This made the Roman cities more productive and changed their society.

Questions to Recap:

1. The first step in making a scientific inquiry is to _____.

2. The concept of science known as "Change, Constancy, and Measurement" explains that _____ of data is important so that ideas can be documented.

3. The following are all characteristics of systems except:
    a. Inputs and outputs
    b. Arranged in a hierarchy
    c. Predict the weather
    d. Organized structure

4. The amount of matter in of an object is called its _____ and the measure of the surface of an object is called its _____.

1.) pose a question 2.) measurement is important for consistency 3.) c 4.) mass, area

Earth Science

Solar system, universe, and the effects of relative positions of the earth, moon, and sun

The Solar System consists of the sun, the planets and their moons, asteroids, meteors, and comets.

The Sun:
The sun is the center of our solar system. It is composed of 75% hydrogen and 25% helium. The energy produced by the sun is the result of a fusion reaction involving hydrogen. The interior portion of the sun is composed of three major zones:

- **Core** – is where nuclear fusion takes place.
- **Radiation Zone** – is the region just outside of the core. This region is mostly electromagnetic radiation.
- **Convection Zone** – is the outside layer of the sun.

The atmosphere of the sun is composed of the corona, the chromospheres, and the photosphere.

- **Corona** – is described as the halo or crown around the sun. This can only be seen during a total solar eclipse.
- **Chromosphere** – is the middle layer of the sun's atmosphere. This is where the light is seen.
- **Photosphere** – is the layer that gives off visible light.

The Inner Planets:
The inner planets are described as small, dense, and rocky. These are also known as the terrestrial planets.

Mercury – is closest to the sun and is the smallest planet. This planet is not much larger than Earth's moon. It has no moon and takes 59 earth days to complete one revolution. During the day, it has a temperature of over 400°C. The night temperature is below -170°C because it has almost no atmosphere.

Venus – is second from the sun and is also known as Earth's twin. It rotates from east to west, which is opposite from most other planets. Venus' atmosphere is composed of very thick clouds made of sulfuric acid, with carbon dioxide near the surface. It traps solar energy and keeps the planet's temperature around 460°C. It also has no moon.

Earth Science

Solar system, universe, and the effects of relative positions of the earth, moon, and sun

Earth – is third from the sun. It is unique in the solar system because it has water, which sustains life. It has seasons and one moon.

Mars – is fourth from the sun. This planet is known as the "Red Planet" because of the red color that comes from the breakdown of iron-rich rocks. Like Earth, Mars has north and south polar ice caps, which are composed of water and carbon dioxide. Mars also has seasons like Earth because it, too, has a tilt. Mars has two moons, Phobos and Deimos.

The Outer Planets:

The outer planets are Jupiter, Saturn, Uranus, and Neptune. These are also known as the "Gas Giants." Unlike the terrestrial planets, the gas giants do not have a solid surface. All of the gas giants have rings and many moons.

Jupiter – is the largest planet in the solar system at twice the size of all the other planets combined. It has over 63 moons. The four largest moons are Io, Ganymede, Callisto, and Europa. Other than its extreme size, Jupiter is known for its "Great Red Spot," a storm that was first seen in the mid-1600s and continues to move around the planet.

Saturn – is the second-largest planet and is known for its amazing ring system. These rings are made of ice and rock. Each ring travels in its own orbit around Saturn. Of all the planets, Saturn is the least dense, having an average density less than water. It has over 47 moons, with the largest named Titan.

Uranus (YOOR uh nus) – is a unique planet in our solar system because it is tilted 90 degrees, so it rotates on its side. It has a small, barely visible ring system that rotates on its side as well. This planet is twice as far from the sun as Saturn; therefore, it is much colder. It has a blue-green appearance from a trace amount of methane. Uranus has over 27 moons.

Neptune – is known as Uranus' twin. This cold, blue planet was discovered because of a mathematical prediction. After scientists noticed Uranus was not following its predicted path, they hypothesized that the gravity of another planet must be affecting it. It has over 13 moons orbiting it.

Earth Science
Solar system, universe, and the effects of relative positions of the earth, moon, and sun

Pluto – is officially classified as a dwarf planet. It has a solid surface like the terrestrial planets. It has three moons in its orbit. Pluto has an elliptical orbit that takes 248 earth years to complete. Because of its elliptical orbit, it is sometimes closer to the sun than Neptune is. *Why change Pluto's classification from planet to dwarf planet?* Because in recent years, astronomers discovered many "Pluto"-like objects. Instead of naming all the objects, they decided to create a new classification. The "dwarf planet" is similar to a planet in the fact that it is round and orbits the sun, but different because there are other things still cluttering the area.

Comets:
Comets are the size of a mountain and are made of ice, dust, and rock particles. Their orbits are usually a long, narrow, elliptical shape. Comets are found in two regions within our solar system – the Kuiper Belt and the Oort Cloud. Comets are composed of a head and a tail. As the comet nears the sun, some of the ice melts and gases are released, causing light. The tail is a trail of gas following behind the comet from the melting ice.

Asteroids:
There is a large space that divides the inner planets from the outer planets. This space is dominated by thousands of small rocky bodies called asteroids. These combine to form the asteroid belt.

Meteoroids:
These are chunks of rock or dust in space. They come from either comets or asteroids. When a meteoroid enters Earth's atmosphere, the friction creates heat and produces a streak of light in the sky. This is a meteor. If a meteoroid hits the surface of the earth, it is classified as a meteorite.

The Universe:
The universe is usually defined as the entirety of everything that exists. This includes all physical matter and energy, galaxies, solar systems, and the other contents of space.

Universe → Galaxies → Solar System

Earth Science

Solar system, universe, and the effects of relative positions of the earth, moon, and sun

Galaxies:
The term galaxy is described as a cluster of billions of stars, star systems, star clusters, dust, and gas bound together by gravity. There are three main types, which are characterized by their shapes: the spiral, the elliptical, and the irregular. Of these three main types, there are sub-categories for each. Our own galaxy, the Milky Way is a "barred-spiral," this means that it is a spiral with a rectangular shaped center rather than the traditional, circular shaped center.

Location of Solar System:
Our solar system is located in the Milky Way Galaxy, on the Orion arm, three-quarters of the way from the center.

Relationship of the Earth, Moon, and Sun:
The movement of the earth and the moon and their relative position to the sun result in: day and night, the seasons, moon phases, eclipses, and tides.

Earth moves through space in two ways: rotation and revolution.
- Rotation – The spinning of the earth, top-like, on its axis. This takes 24 hours.
- Revolution – The movement of an object (earth) around another (sun).

The path the earth follows is called its 'orbit'.

Earth Science

Solar system, universe, and the effects of relative positions of the earth, moon, and sun

Seasons:

Earth experiences seasons because of the 23.5-degree tilt from the vertical. Because of this tilt, at certain times of the year, the earth is either angled towards or away from the sun. This either increases or decreases the amount of light energy the area receives. If there were no tilt, there would be no seasons.

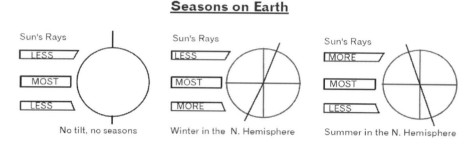

Moon Phases:

The alignment of the moon, sun, and earth cause moon phases. The moon phase seen on Earth depends on how much of the sunlit side of the moon is facing the earth. The moon cycle takes 29.5 days. Like the earth, it rotates and revolves.

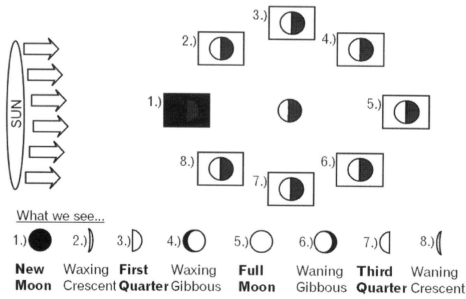

The Moon completes one rotation and one revolution in the same amount of time, making a day and a year the same length. For this reason the same side of the moon always faces the earth.

Earth Science

Composition, structure, and processes of the earth's lithosphere, hydrosphere, and atmosphere, and the interactions among these systems

Lithosphere – describes earth's rocky, outer surface made of the crust and the upper mantle.

Characteristics of Soil:
- Soil is the loose, weathered material, such as rock particles, minerals, decayed organic material, water, and air.
- Soil is found on the earth's surface. This is where plants grow. The word soil describes clay, silt, sand, and gravel.
- Soil is classified by its particle size.
- Soil is classified into major groups based on climate, plants, and its composition.
- Soil is constantly being formed as rock is broken down through weathering or when bedrock is exposed. This new soil is mixed with other minerals.

Soil Formation:
Soil develops in layers called soil horizons. The top layer is the **A-horizon** and is made up of topsoil, which is a dark brown soil. This is a mixture of humus (plant and animal decay), clay, and other minerals. The middle layer is the **B-horizon**, which is composed of clay and other particles but little to no humus. This area is also known as subsoil. The bottom layer next to the bedrock is called the **C-horizon** and contains only weathered rocks.

Note: Soil forms fastest in warm, rainy climates.

Earth Science

Composition, structure, and processes of the earth's lithosphere, hydrosphere, and atmosphere, and the interactions among these systems

Rocks:

Rocks are composed of mixtures of minerals and other materials. Some rocks, however, contain a single mineral. To classify rocks, geologists observe the rock's mineral composition, color, and texture.

Geologists classify rocks into three major categories: igneous, sedimentary, or metamorphic rocks. They are also organized by particle size.

- Igneous rocks – form from cooling magma or lava. These rocks are classified by where they occur, texture, and chemical composition. An example is granite.
- Sedimentary rocks – form when particles of other rocks or the remains of animals and plants are cemented together. Examples are flint and sandstone.
- Metamorphic rocks – form from existing rocks that are changed through heat pressure or chemical reaction. This almost always takes place deep within the earth. Examples are slate and marble.

The Rock Cycle:

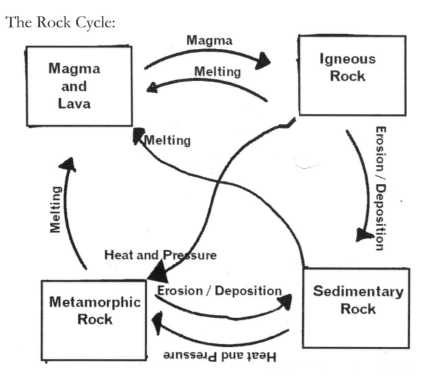

Earth Science

Composition, structure, and processes of the earth's lithosphere, hydrosphere, and atmosphere, and the interactions among these systems

Minerals:
A mineral is a naturally occurring, inorganic solid that has a crystal structure and a definite chemical composition. For something to be considered a mineral, it must exhibit **ALL** five characteristics.
1. **Naturally Occurring** – For a substance to be classified as a mineral, it must be formed by processes in the natural world.
2. **Inorganic** – To be a mineral, a substance must be inorganic. This means that the mineral cannot form from material that was once living. A common example used is coal. It was once a living thing; therefore, coal is not considered to be a mineral.
3. **Solid** – To be considered a mineral, it must be a solid with definite volume and shape.
4. **Crystal Structure** – The particles of a mineral line up in a pattern that repeats over and over.
5. **Definite Chemical Composition** – To be a mineral, it must always contain a certain element or elements in definite proportions.

Each mineral has specific characteristics and/or properties. These are used to identify each mineral.

Hydrosphere – is all of the earth's water.
The water cycle is the continuous process by which water moves from the surface of the earth to the atmosphere and back. There are three major steps in the water cycle: evaporation, condensation, and precipitation. There is no beginning or end, and it is driven by the energy of the sun.

Steps of the Water Cycle:
- Water Evaporates – Water changes to water vapor by evaporation. Water is consistently being evaporated from lakes, streams, and the oceans. Plants are also major contributors to this step because they draw water from the ground and release it into the air as water vapor.
- Cloud Formation – As water vapor enters the atmosphere, it moves up. As the water vapor moves higher, the air cools. Cooler air cannot hold as much water vapor, so the vapor condenses together around dust particles and bonds together to form clouds.
- Precipitation – is rain, snow, sleet, or hail. As clouds form and grow larger, they cannot hold all the water so it falls back to earth.

Earth Science

Composition, structure, and processes of the earth's lithosphere, hydrosphere, and atmosphere, and the interactions among these systems

The Distribution of Water on Earth's Surface:

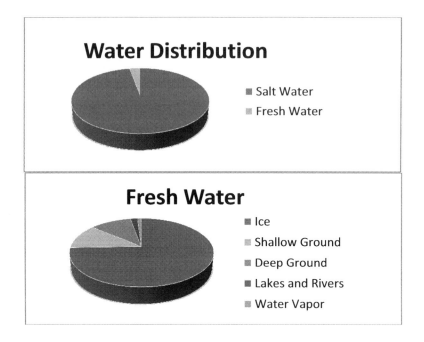

Three-fourths of the world is covered by water. Approximately ninety-seven percent of the water on Earth is in the oceans. The remaining three percent is freshwater. Approximately seventy-five percent of the available freshwater is frozen in polar ice caps that cover Antarctica and Greenland, as well as huge icebergs and ice sheets at the North and South Poles.

Twenty-three percent of the water on Earth is found in the ground as shallow or deep ground water. The remaining water is in lakes, rivers, and water vapor.

Earth Science

Composition, structure, and processes of the earth's lithosphere, hydrosphere, and atmosphere, and the interactions among these systems

Atmosphere:

Composition – The earth's atmosphere is mainly composed of nitrogen, oxygen, carbon dioxide, and water vapor, as well as other liquids and solids.

- Nitrogen – is the most abundant, making up about 78% of the atmosphere. Nitrogen is constantly moving in a cycle from the air into the soil, then into living things, then back into the air. This is known as the nitrogen cycle.
- Oxygen – is a vital component in most all life processes, however, it makes up only 21% of the air around us.
- Other gases – account for the other 1% of gases. These include: argon, carbon dioxide, neon, helium, methane, krypton, and hydrogen; however, argon makes up .93% of the 1%.
- Water Vapor (water in its gas form) – The amount of water vapor in an area plays an important role in that area's weather.
- Particles – are all around us and include things such as smoke, salt, and dust.

Structure – The atmosphere is composed of four main layers. Scientists differentiate these layers based on the temperature within each of the layers. The layers are the troposphere, the stratosphere, the mesosphere, and the thermosphere.

- Troposphere – is the layer closest to earth. This layer is also the thinnest layer. While this is the smallest of the four layers, it contains almost all of the mass for the entire atmosphere. This is where the earth's weather occurs.
- Stratosphere – is the second layer of the atmosphere and contains the ozone layer. The stratosphere is unique in that the upper stratosphere is warmer than the lower stratosphere. This is because the ozone layer acts as a blanket, keeping some of the heat out.
- Mesosphere – is the third layer of the atmosphere. This layer provides the earth's surface protection from meteoroids.
- Thermosphere – is the outer layer and has no definite thickness because it extends into space. The air in the thermosphere is thin and receives the most direct solar rays.

Earth Science

Composition, structure, and processes of the earth's lithosphere, hydrosphere, and atmosphere, and the interactions among these systems

Temperature, wind, and humidity are the major factors that influence weather.
- Temperature – is the measure of the amount of energy in the air molecules.
- Wind – is a horizontal movement of air from high to low pressure.
- Humidity – is the amount of water vapor present in the air.
    - Relative Humidity – is the amount of water vapor present in the air compared to the amount needed for saturation at a temperature. This means that as the temperature increases, the air can hold more water.
    - Dew Point – When the temperature drops at night, the air cools and can hold less water. The point or temperature at which the water vapor transitions back into water is called the dew point. The water vapor condenses and falls to the ground. This is called dew and, if it freezes, it is called frost.

Clouds – are the result of condensed water vapor in the atmosphere. Cold air holds less water vapor than warm air. As the air cools, the amount of water vapor a cloud can hold decreases. The water vapor will condense into water droplets or ice crystals. This process causes rain, snow, and dew. Clouds are the result of the amount of humidity or water vapor that is present in the atmosphere. Clouds can influence the temperature of an area. They also sometimes bring rain to an area.

As the temperature rises, the amount of humidity rises as well because water is turned into water vapor. As the percent of water vapor increases, the water vapor starts to condense together and form clouds. As these clouds grow, they block sunlight from reaching the earth's surface. This causes the air to cool. Once the air cools, the clouds lose the ability to hold as much water. The result is precipitation. Wind speed plays a vital role in the formation of clouds. The amount of wind can control the amount of humidity present in the atmosphere.

Earth Science

Composition, structure, and processes of the earth's lithosphere, hydrosphere, and atmosphere, and the interactions among these systems

Fronts – are colliding air masses that can form four kinds of fronts: cold, warm, stationary, and occluded.
- **Cold Front** – results when a fast moving cold air mass overtakes a warm air mass. As a rule, cold fronts move fast and can cause sudden weather changes resulting in thunderstorms. Once a cold front moves through, it leaves colder, drier air, clear skies, wind, and a lower temperature.
- **Warm Front** – results when a fast moving warm air mass overtakes a slower moving cold air mass. After a warm front passes, the resulting weather is usually warm and humid.
- **Stationary Front** – results when a warm air mass meets a cold air mass. The result is large amounts of precipitation for many days.
- **Occluded Front** – results when a warm air mass is caught between two cooler air masses. The cool air mass cools the warm air. The result is cloudy weather with possible precipitation.

Thunderstorms – form in cumulonimbus clouds, which usually form on hot humid afternoons or along cold fronts. The warm humid air moves fast as the air cools, forming a dense thunderhead. The result is heavy rain, lightning, thunder, and hail.

Tornadoes – are a rapidly whirling, funnel-shaped cloud. They develop in thunderstorms, and are common in the same locations and during the same seasons as the thunderstorms.

Hurricanes – form over warm oceans as an area of low pressure or tropical disturbance. As it grows and moves, it gathers strength over warm humid oceans and becomes a tropical storm, which may become a hurricane. As the wind speed increases, so does the category of the hurricane.

Earth Science
Tools for observing, measuring, predicting, and communicating weather data

When meteorologists predict the weather they use a series of devices and steps in order to create an accurate prediction of the upcoming weather.

Observe:
- Doppler Radar – is a computed image of the current weather. Radar is useful for watching developing storms and cloud formation.
- Meteorologists – study the causes of weather and try to predict it.

Measure:
- Rain Gauge – measures the amount of rain.
- Sling Psychomotor – measures the amount of relative humidity.
- Barometer – measures air pressure.
- Anemometer – measures wind speed.
- Wind vane – shows the direction the wind is blowing.

Predicting:
Meteorologists use things like weather maps, charts of weather, and computer simulators to evaluate weather data in order to make predictions. Today, data is compiled and computer simulations are used to give weather predictions.

Communicating:
Weather is communicated via the internet, the Weather Channel, local network stations, and newspaper articles.

Earth Science

Natural and human-caused constructive and destructive processes

Mountains – The result of the collision of two plates and from weak areas in the crust. Mountains are shaped from erosion and weathering but are built through plate tectonics.

Canyons – The result of erosion, usually a river, which makes a path in the surface of the earth.

Erosion – The removal of the weathered materials with wind, water, and ice.

Weathering – The breakdown of rock and other materials.
- Mechanical Weathering – Materials are broken down through physically freezing and thawing or animals' actions.
- Chemical Weathering – Materials are broken down through a chemical change with water, elements, and acid rain.
  - Water – dissolves chemical binders.
  - Elements – can cause rust or create carbonic acid that erodes limestone.
  - Acid Rain – Pollution mixes with rain and causes rapid chemical weathering.

Plate Tectonics:
This is a widely accepted theory that states that pieces of the earth's lithosphere are in slow, constant motion, driven by the convection currents in the mantle. The theory of plate tectonics explains the movement of the earth's plates. This movement results in the formation of volcanoes, mountain ranges (above and below the ocean's surface), and deep trenches in the ocean. The edges of the plates run deep into the lithosphere. Faults are where the plates come together.

Earth Science
Natural and human-caused constructive and destructive processes

There are three kinds of plate boundaries: divergent, convergent, and transform.

Divergent Boundary – is the place where two plates move apart. These boundaries occur along mid-ocean ridges where sea floor spreading happens. Examples: the Red Sea Rift and East Pacific Rise.

Convergent Boundary – is the place where two plates come together in a collision. This type of collision results in mountain building as well as trenches. Examples: the Himalayas, volcanoes of the Pacific.

Transform Boundary – is a place where two plates slip past each other in opposite directions. Examples: North American Queen Charlotte Fault.

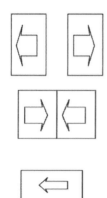

Results of Plate Movement:

Earthquake – is the shaking and trembling of the earth as plates move. These can be so mild that they are not felt, or so intense that the surface of the earth can be changed.

Volcanoes – shape the Earth's crust. These are weak places in the crust where molten material or magma comes to the surface. Many volcanoes are found along plate boundaries. The most well-known volcanic area is the "Ring of Fire." This area outlines the Pacific Ocean. Volcanoes are found on divergent boundaries and converging boundaries. Some volcanoes, however, occur nowhere near plate boundaries. These are called 'hotspots'. The Hawaiian Islands are an example of this.

Types of Volcanoes:

There are four types of volcanoes: shield, cinder cone, composite, and lava plateaus.

- Shield Volcanoes – are low, flat, slow erupting volcanoes that gradually build; Hawaii is made of these.
- Cinder Cone Volcanoes – are violent erupting volcanoes. These produce ash, cinders, and bombs. The materials build up in a steep, cone-shaped hill.
- Composite Volcanoes – are tall, cone-shaped volcanic mountains with alternating layers of ash and lava.
- Lava Plateaus – are the volcanic eruptions of lava from high level areas called plateaus.

Earth Science
Fossil formation and how they provide evidence of past organisms

Fossils – An animal or plant dies and most of the time the remains are eaten or decompose. However, sometimes the remains get buried by mud or soil, and harden into fossils. Over time, the bones or original material decay. During this time, water and minerals seep into the impression left by the original material, replacing it and hardening over time. What is left is a rock in the shape of the plant or animal.

Fossils are traces of past life found in rocks. Scientists use this information to study the past.

Fossils are usually found in sedimentary rock found in marine or prehistoric marine environments. Fossils are more often found in these environments because they are less likely to be disturbed.

Earth Science

Questions to Recap:

1. Name three of the outer planets in our solar system.

2. What is a dwarf planet

3. Where is the earth's solar system located?

4. Coal is not a mineral because it is _____.

5. Which of the following is not a main layer in the earth's atmosphere?
    a. Mesosphere
    b. Biosphere
    c. Stratosphere
    d. Troposphere

6. Meteorologists use a sling psychomotor to measure the amount of
_____.

7. All of the following are types of volcanoes except:
    a. Cinder cone
    b. Lava plateaus
    c. Compound
    d. Shield

8. Match each type of rock below to the category it belongs to:
    a. Marble   1. Sedimentary
    b. Granite   2. Metamorphic
    c. Flint   3. Igneous

1.) Jupiter, Saturn, Uranus, Neptune 2.) a small planet that has many other small planet like objects around it 3.) in the Milky Way Galaxy, on the Orion Arm ⅔ of the way from the center 4.) organic 5.) b 6.) relative humidity 7.) c 8.) a-2, b-2, c-3

Physical Science

The structure and properties of matter

Matter is defined as anything that has weight and occupies space; it is the stuff around us. There are three states/properties of matter: solid, liquid, and gas.

Physical Properties – The characteristics that can be observed or measured without altering the identity (chemical composition) of the material. Matter has mass, which is the amount of matter in an object, and volume, which is the amount of space the matter occupies.

Physical properties include, but are not limited to: appearance, boiling point, color, density, melting point, odor, and texture.

Vocabulary Related to Matter:
- Mass – is the amount of matter within an object.
- Weight – is the measure of the gravitational pull on an object.
- Volume – is the amount of space that an object takes up.
- Density – is the concentration of matter in an object; as temperature increases, an object's density decreases, and as an object's temperature decreases, density increases.
- Freezing Point – is when a substance changes from a liquid to a solid; for example, the freezing point of water is 0°C or 32°F.
- Boiling Point – is when a substance changes from a liquid to a gas; for example, the boiling point of water is 100°C or 212°F.

Physical Science
The structure and properties of matter

Structure and Properties of Matter:
All matter is composed of atoms, which combine to form molecules. All matter has density, a freezing point, and a melting point.

- **Atoms** – are the smallest unit of an element.

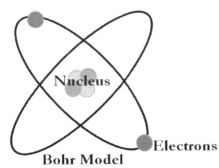

Structure of an Atom:
Nucleus – center of an atom, composed of protons and neutrons.
Proton – subatomic particle with positive charge.
Neutron – subatomic particle with no charge.
Electron – subatomic particle in a negative charge; makes the clouds.

- **Element** – a substance made up of only one kind of atom.
- **Molecule** – a grouping of two or more atoms joined together.

Pure Substances – describes matter that is composed of the same type of atom. When all of the atoms are alike, the matter is called an element.

- **Element** – a material that is made up of only one type of atom.
- **Compound** – results when atoms of different elements bond.

Impure Substance – is a mixture or a combination of two or more substances in which each substance retains its own properties. A mixture can be separated through physical means. An example is saltwater and sand.

- **Heterogeneous Mixture** – A mixture of different components in which the different substances can be seen, like oil and water.
- **Homogeneous Mixture** – A mixture in which the individual components are mixed so well that the composition is the same throughout.

Item	Characteristic	Example
Element	Made of one kind of atom	Carbon
Compound	Made of two or more kinds of atoms/elements	Water
Mixture	Combination of two or more elements or compounds but they keep their physical properties	Salt and Pepper

Physical Science
Physical and chemical changes

Physical Change:
This is a change in the size, shape, color, and state of matter, but when the identity of the substance does not change. The most common example includes the three states of matter: solid, liquid, and gas. For example, ice is placed in a pot on the stove; the ice melts to water and then turns to steam.
Cutting and Physical Change – Metal is still metal when cut.

Chemical Change:
The change of substances to different substances; for example, when something is burned or it rusts.

When iron is exposed to air, it rusts and begins to change into a new substance. When gas is burned, elements are removed/burned off and a new substance emerges.

Physical Science
Conservation of matter and conservation of energy

Law of Conservation of Matter – Matter is neither created nor destroyed during a physical or chemical change.

Law of Conservation of Energy – Energy can neither be created nor destroyed; energy can change forms.

Physical Science
Forms of energy, processes of energy transfer, and the interactions of energy and matter

Types of Energy:
Energy is defined as the ability to cause change in matter.
- **Kinetic Energy** – is energy in motion or any matter in motion. Sound energy, light energy, mechanical energy, thermal energy, and electric energy are all forms of kinetic energy.
- **Potential Energy** – is energy due to location. Chemical energy, gravitational potential energy, and elastic potential energy are all forms of potential energy.

Physical Science

Forms of energy, processes of energy transfer, and the interactions of energy and matter

Forms of Energy:

Chemical Energy – is energy released or absorbed due to a chemical reaction. It can be in the form of light, heat, sound, or electricity. An example is when wood is burned, it releases heat and light.

Electrical Energy – is the result of a motor, which is driven by many different means. For example, most electricity is produced through the burning of fossil fuel; however, it is also produced in hydroelectric and nuclear power plants.

Mechanical Energy – is the total amount of energy in a system, including both kinetic energy and potential energy. An example of mechanical energy is a swing moving back and forth; it transforms from potential and kinetic energy over and over.

Heat Energy – is also known as thermal energy; heat speeds up molecules. Heat energy can be used to heat water to create steam, which, in turn, can create electric energy, or geothermal heat is captured.

Electromagnetic Energy – This energy is also known as the electromagnetic spectrum. It includes radio waves, infrared, visible light, X-rays, and gamma rays. These are used in many aspects of our daily lives.

- Radio Waves – include a.m. waves, f.m. waves, radar, and microwaves; deliver music and news and warm our food.
- Infrared Radiation – used to warm and dehydrate food.
- Visible Radiation – visible light; the only part of the electromagnetic spectrum we can see.
- Ultraviolet Radiation – used to kill microorganisms on food without cooking it and to sterilize medical instruments.
- X-Rays – used to take images of bones.
- Gamma Rays – used to kill cancerous cells in the body.

Light Energy – a type of energy that can travel though the vacuum of space or through matter.

Sound Energy – carried by vibrating matter. This is used for Doppler radar and sonar.

Solar Energy – Energy from the sun is used in many ways. We use it to make energy for our homes, and plants use it to make food; its uses are almost limitless.

Physical Science

Forms of energy, processes of energy transfer, and the interactions of energy and matter

Interaction of Energy and Matter:

Conduction – is the transfer of energy through matter by direct contact of particles. Energy is transferred when particles moving at different speeds bump into each other. Conduction occurs in solids, liquids, and gases. However, energy conducts better with solids because it requires contact. Matter must be present.

Convection – is the transfer of energy by the bulk movement of matter. In convection, fluid particles move from one location to another, taking energy with them. As heat is added, the particles move faster. Matter must be present.

Radiation – is the transfer of energy in the form of waves. No matter is needed for radiation to occur.

Physical Science

Types of forces and effects on the position, motion, and behavior of objects

Types of Forces

Contact Forces:

Friction – is a result of contact and is the force that opposes the push or pull of objects.

Distance Forces:

Magnetism – is the force of alteration between magnetic objects.

Gravity – is the force exerted by every object in the universe on every other object. The amount of gravity depends on the mass of the object and the distance between them. For example, the moon has less mass than the earth; therefore, it has less gravity. This means you will weigh less on the moon; however, your mass is the same on the moon and earth.

Electrostatic – is the force that holds electric charges together when a negatively charged particle attracts to a positively charged particle.

Physical Science

Types of forces and effects on the position, motion, and behavior of objects

Motion:
This is determined by one's position in reference to an object. The motion of an object depends on your motion while you are observing an object. Motion can be described in terms of speed and velocity.
- Speed – the measurement of the distance an object moves in a certain amount of time.
- Velocity – an object's speed in a certain direction. Any change in velocity is called acceleration.

The Laws of Motion:
   Newton's First Law of Motion – states that an object at rest will stay at rest, and an object in motion will continue moving in a straight line at a constant speed until an outside force acts on it. This is also known as the law of inertia.
   Newton's Second Law – states that a net force acting on an object causes the object to accelerate in the direction of the force. Acceleration is determined by the size of the force and the mass of the object. This law uses this equation: *Force = mass x acceleration*.
   Newton's Third Law – describes action/reaction pairs, or *for every action there is an equal and opposite reaction.*
      Examples: A person leaps from a boat and his or her foot pushes the boat away during the jump. A person is jumping on a pogo stick; the spring presses down and forces the person up.

Balanced and Unbalanced Forces:
   Balanced Force – forces that are equal in size and in opposite directions; as a result, these forces cancel each other out.
   Unbalanced Force – forces that are not equal in size or opposite in directions; these will change an object's motion.
   Net Force – the combined amount of forces.

Physical Science
Simple machines

Machines:
A **machine** is a device that makes work easier. There are simple and complex machines.

Simple Machines – do work with only one movement. There are six types of simple machines: lever, pulley, wheel and axle, incline plane, screw, and wedge.
- Lever – is a bar that is free to pivot about a fixed point, or fulcrum.
- Pulley – is a wheel with grooves, with a rope or a chain running along the grooves.
- Wheel and Axle – is a machine consisting of two wheels of different sizes that rotate together. Gears are an example.
- Incline Plane – is a sloping surface used to raise an object. An example is a ramp.
- Screw – is an incline plane wrapped in a spiral around a cylindrical post.
- Wedge – is an incline plane with two sloping sides. Examples are chisels, knives, and ax blades.

These machines all make work more effective by focusing the energy.

Compound Machine – is a combination of two or more simple machines.

Physical Science
Characteristics of light, sound, electricity, and magnetism

Light:
  Reflection – when a wave of light strikes a surface and bounces off/mirrors. Reflection of light is used in scanning or three-dimensional microscopes.
  Refraction – when a wave is bent (this changes the direction of the wave/lens). This is used in binoculars, microscopes, and telescopes to make small objects more visible by bending a light source. This is also how we see color.
  Diffusion – when a wave strikes a surface and moves through windows, blinds, or lamp shades. This can be used to make a bright light more bearable for your eyes. Our pupils also help us, by adjusting to allow more or less light in.

Physical Science

Characteristics of light, sound, electricity, and magnetism

Light (cont'd.)
   Mirror – is a flat surface with a reflective coating on the front or back. Light enters and is reflected back at the same angle.

Lenses are Concave or Convex:
Concave Lenses – are thinner in the middle and thicker at the edges. Light enters and is dispersed out. Concave lenses make things look smaller so you can see the entire thing, like looking through a peephole or binoculars.

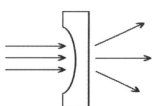

Convex Lenses – are thicker in the middle than the edge. Light enters and is focused together. These are used in magnifying glasses.

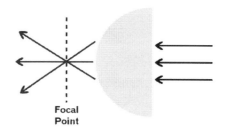

Prisms – take white light and refract the wavelengths individually. You can see seven colors: red, orange, yellow, green, blue, indigo, and violet.

Sound:
Sound – describes vibrations your brain recognizes as sound. It travels in waves. Hearing sound involves three stages: the ear gathers and amplifies the compression wave with the mechanisms of the ear, the waves are processed into nerve impulses, and they are decoded in the brain.
- Echoes – are the reflection of sound bouncing off a wall. The time delay is from the extra distance divided by the speed at which sound travels.

Pitch – is the highness or lowness of a sound.

Physical Science
Characteristics of light, sound, electricity, and magnetism

Electricity:
Electrical energy is used to create many other types of energy. We use electricity to create heat, like with an electric heater or stove. This occurs when electricity passes through a circuit: – in the circuit there is a resistor, and this resistor slows the electrons. This slowing causes the electrons to build up and create heat. Light is created this way as well. We use electricity to create mechanical energy, like in an electric blender. We also use electricity to create sound.

Electric Current – the flow of electrons. These currents flow from power stations and into homes. Electric current is used to power our lives.

Electric Circuit – the path through which electrons flow. There are two kinds: series and parallel.
  Components of a circuit: power source – battery, load – light bulb or device, switch – control device that opens and closes the circuit, and connectors – wires that connect resistance to the source of electricity.

Series Circuit – is a single path for the flow of electrons in a series circuit. If one bulb/device burns out, all of the other bulbs will stop working because the circuit is broken.

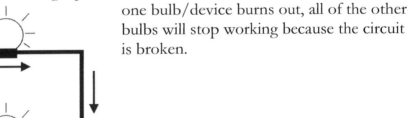

Parallel Circuit – Each bulb/device is on its own path. So if one device goes out the others continue to work.

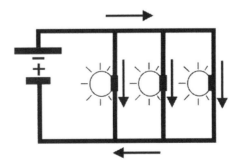

Physical Science
Characteristics of light, sound, electricity, and magnetism

Components Used with Electricity:
  Conductors –These are used when we want the flow of electrons to continue; increases the flow of electrons.
  Insulators –These are used when we want the flow of electrons to stop.

Magnetism:

Magnetism – is a property of some matter where the force of attraction or repulsion is between unlike or like poles. Magnetic forces are strongest near the ends, known as magnetic poles.
- All magnets have two opposite poles. These poles are known as north (N) and south (S) poles. They always have one north and one south pole; even if we cute a magnet in half it forms a new north and south pole.
- Opposite poles attract each other and like poles repel each other.
- Magnets also have fields. This is the area around the magnet where the magnetic forces act.

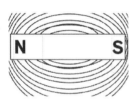

Characteristics of Magnets:
- Opposite poles attract, like poles repel.
- Magnetic fields are the regions around the magnet where a magnetic force is present.

Physical Science

Questions to Recap:

1. The freezing point of a substance is when it changes from a liquid to a _____ and the boiling point of a substance is when it changes from a liquid to a _____.

2. Light energy, thermal energy, and sound energy are all forms of _____ energy.

3. Newton's Third Law states that, for every action, there is an equal and _____ reaction.

4. Which of the following is not an example of a simple machine:
    a. Incline plane
    b. Wedge
    c. Bicycle
    d. Pulley

5. All magnets have a _____ pole and a _____ pole.

6. In a series circuit, if one bulb burns out, they will _____ working and in a parallel circuit, if one bulb burns out, they will _____ to work.

7. An atom consists of all of the following except:
    a. Electron
    b. Proton
    c. Neutron
    d. All of the above
    e. None of the above

1.) solid, gas 2.) kinetic 3.) opposite 4.) c 5.) north, south 6.) stop, continue 7.) d

Life Science

Living versus nonliving things

To be considered a living thing, it must meet all of the following characteristics:

- Living things have a complex organization in the form of a cell or cells. Living things **are made of cells**.
- Living things **obtain and use energy** through metabolism or photosynthesis.
- Living things **grow and develop**. To do this, organisms take things from their environment and reorganize them to build new cells. For example, plants take in minerals from soil and build new cells.
- Living things **reproduce**. All living things have the ability to make copies of themselves through asexual or sexual reproduction.
- Living things **respond to their environment** or their external environment. For example, leaves lift toward the sun. Or, an animal may fly away when you approach.
- Living things **adapt to their environment**. Living things can change locations if an environment becomes uninhabitable, or a plant can grow taller to gain more exposure to the sun.

If something does not meet all of these criteria, it is considered to be nonliving.

Life Science
Different types of organisms and methods of classification

Domain – is the highest taxonomic rank of organisms It includes three domains: Archaea, Bacteria, and Eukarya. This is also known as the tree of life.

Organism Classification System:
- **Kingdom** – This is the second layer of organization. It consists of Bacteria, Archaea, Protista, Fungi, Plantae, and Animalia. Organisms are grouped into these kingdoms based on four characteristics: presence of a nucleus, single-celled or many celled, ability to make food, and ability to move. Humans belong to the kingdom 'animalia'.
- **Phylum** – is a group of organisms with a measure of evolutionary similarities. We belong to the phylum 'chordata'.
- **Class** – We belong to the class 'mammalia'.
- **Order** – We belong to the order 'primata'.
- **Family** – We belong to the family 'hominid'.
- **Genus** – We belong to the genus 'Hom'.
- **Species** – Being the smallest, most specific group, we belong to the species 'sapiens'.

Six-Kingdom System:
Protists – are found along the evolutionary track. They share characteristics with fungi, plants, and animals. These organisms, however, do not have all the defining characteristics of the defining groups (that is, they are not as far down the evolutionary road as the rest).

Fungi – were once classified as plants, but we now know they are much different for many reasons. The main reason is that, unlike plants, fungi do not make their own food. Also they do not have specialized organs, such as leaves and roots.

Life Science

Different types of organisms and methods of classification

Plants – make their own food through photosynthesis; this is the defining factor for this group. Plants can be broken down into subgroups.
- Nonvascular Plants:
  These are plants without vessels or tubes to carry water and nutrients throughout the plant. These plants move nutrients from cell to cell; because of this, these plants tend to be smaller. An example is peat moss.
- Vascular Plant:
  Seedless Vascular Plants – are similar to the nonvascular plants in appearance, however, they can grow larger because they have a more efficient way to transport nutrients. A major example of this group is the ferns.
  Seeded Vascular Plants – have two major groups: the gymnosperm and the angiosperm.
    - Gymnosperm – are plants with seeds that are not protected by a fruit. Some examples are pines and palms.
    - Angiosperms – are plants with seeds that are protected by a fruit. These are flowering plants such as oak trees, lemon trees, and corn.

Animals – are advanced organisms that have no cell wall, are multi-celled, cannot make their own food, and have specialized organs for life processes. There are many groups and categories for this kingdom. One of the most basic classification stipulations is the presence of a backbone. Some examples include:
- Invertebrates – animals that lack a backbone or spine. Invertebrates make up over 95% of all animals and include: flat worms, ribbon worms, earthworms, segmented worms, snails, bi-vales, squid, round worms, and arthropods (insects, crustaceans, spiders).
- Vertebrates – animals that have backbones or a spinal column.
    - Cyclostomes – jawless fish
    - Bony Fish – grouper, bass, catfish (have bones)
    - Sharks – full cartilage skeleton; bull shark, tiger shark
    - Rays – electric ray, saw fish, skates, sting ray
    - Amphibians – frogs, toads, salamanders (breathe in water to start life, breathe air later, cold blooded)
    - Reptiles – snakes, lizards, turtles (cold blooded, lay eggs)
    - Mammals – humans, bears (warm blooded, have mamma glands)
    - Birds – hawk, chickens, ostrich (lay eggs, wings, bipedal)

Life Science
Basic needs, characteristics, structures, and life processes of organisms

Physiological Processes of Plants:

Photosynthesis – The process that plants use to take energy from the sun and create food for energy. The byproduct is oxygen.

Respiration – is the process of breaking down food to release energy. This is the opposite of photosynthesis; it uses oxygen and food to produce energy for cells. The byproducts of respiration are carbon dioxide and water.

Transpiration – is the process when water is released into the atmosphere through plants' stomata of leaves.

Reproduction – is the process of combining genetic material using spores, seeds protected by cones and fruit.

Response to Stimuli – Plants respond to stimuli in many ways. They will grow toward the light. They will usually grow up, no matter their position.

Physiological Processes of Animals:

Respiration – The process of bringing oxygen-rich air into the lungs. On the breath in, air is passed into the circulatory system and the oxygen is used by body processes. Then, carbon dioxide is excreted out through the circulatory system and then the lungs on the breath out.

Reproduction – The process of creating new life by combining egg and sperm to carry genetic information.

Digestion – The process of breaking down food both chemically and mechanically by means of chewing and churning. Food passes through the digestive track and nutrients are extracted for use in the body, while waste is passed from the body.

Circulation – The process of carrying blood through the body. The blood provides transport for nutrients, oxygen, and waste into and out of the body.

Life Science
Basic needs, characteristics, structures, and life processes of organisms

Cells are described as the building blocks of life, and this is true in animals. Cells build tissues, which combine to form organs. These organs together form organ systems. The organ systems come together to protect the cells, remove waste, and create fuel from food.

- Cells – There are over 100 trillion cells in the body and over 100 different kinds of cells.
- Tissues – are groups of cells that are the same type and perform a particular function. There are four types: epithelial (skin, stomach lining), nerve (nerves, brain, spinal cord), connective (bone, blood), and muscle (smooth, skeletal, cardiac).
- Organs – are body structures that are made of several types of tissue. Example: The heart is made of cardiac tissue and beats using nerve tissue.
- Organ System – a group of organs that work together to carry out functions.

Life Science
Heredity and life cycles

Heredity:
Heredity – the passing of traits from parents to offspring. Traits are inherited through alleles, or the different version of a trait. Gregor Mendel discovered the basic laws of genetics through experiments during his time as a monk.

- There are two main types of alleles: dominate and recessive.
- The dominate allele is the one that is visible.
- The recessive allele is the one we cannot see or that is not represented.
- The offspring of an allele cross can be determined used a Punnett Square.

Evolution:
The change in the hereditary features of a species over time.

Natural Selection:
Darwin's Theory of Evolution, which says that the organism that is best adapted to the environment will survive long enough to reproduce.

Life Science

Interactions of organisms and the flow of energy and matter within an ecosystem

Ecosystems:
Ecosystem – is a community and the physical environment of an area.
Community – is all of the populations of organisms living in an environment.
Population – is all of the individuals of the same species living in the same environment.

Each ecosystem is composed of **habitats**, which are the locations where the populations live. Each population has a role or niche in the habitat.

Energy is Transferred through Ecosystem:
Food Chain – the path of energy through the trophic levels of an ecosystem.

Food Web – the interconnected food chain found within an ecosystem.

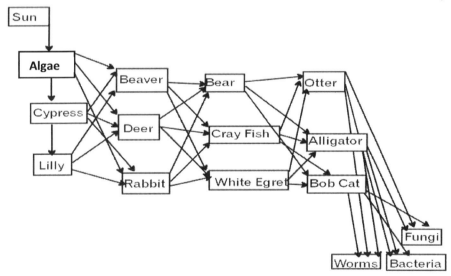

Life Science

Interactions of organisms and the flow of energy and matter within an ecosystem

Energy Flows through an Ecosystem:
Producers – are the organisms in an ecosystem that are first to capture the power of the sun through photosynthesis. Examples include plants, some bacteria, and algae.
Consumers – are the organisms that consume plants or other organisms to obtain energy. Examples include fish, opossum, and alligators.
Decomposers – are organisms that cause decay; their job is to rid the planet of waste. Examples include fungi, worms, and buzzards.

Long-Term Interactions between Two Different Types of Organisms is Called Symbiosis:
Types of Symbiosis:
- **Mutualism** – relationship where both organisms benefit from the grouping.
  Example: shark and cleaner fish – the shark is cleaned and the fish get food to eat.
- **Commensalism** – relationship between organisms where one benefits and the other is unaffected.
  Example: a cow bird eating bugs off of a cow.
- **Parasitism** – The parasite benefits at the expense of a host.
  Example: tapeworm.

Life Science

Effects of humans on the environment

Natural events such as flooding, hurricanes, and drought change the environment. This can cause population decrease. However, the environment is not the main culprit; mankind has a profound effect on organisms and the environment. People deplete the resources found within the environment. Mankind is responsible for the depletion of entire species and vast amounts of resources.

Life Science

Factors that affect the survival or extinction of organisms

Extinction – the last individual in the population dies; the organism is gone forever.

Endangered – means the organisms have a population so small that they are likely to become extinct if steps to save them are not taken right away.

Threatened – The organisms are protected by strict laws, and hunting is limited with strict regulations.

Questions to Recap:

1. Living things have all of the following characteristics except:
   a. Grow and develop
   b. Adapt to their environment
   c. Make their own food
   d. Reproduce

2. Humans belong to the Kingdom known as _____.

3. The following are all examples of vertebrates except:
   a. Worms
   b. Reptiles
   c. Squid
   d. Cyclostomes

4. _____ is the process of carrying blood through the body.

5. What is Darwin's Theory of Evolution?

1.) c   2.) animalia   3.) c   4.) circulation   5.) is the change in a species over time

Heath, Physical Education, and the Arts

This section is organized according to the frameworks available in PDF format from the GACE website www.gace.nesinc.com. There are three objectives for this section.

Items in this section:
- ☑ Health and Safety
- ☑ Physical Education
- ☑ Art

Health and Safety

The primary functions, processes, and development

Systems	Components	Tasks/Functions
Skeletal	Bones, skulls, and cartilage	Protects organs and provides support
Circulatory	Heart, blood vessels, and blood	Transports everything to and from cells
Endocrine	Pituitary, adrenal, thyroid, and other ductless glands	Hormone control
Nervous	Nerves, sense organs, brain, and spinal cord	Controls the activities of the body
Respiratory	Lungs and trachea	Captures oxygen and expels other gases
Immune	Lymph nodes, lymphocytes, and spleen	Removes/filters out bad or harmful foreign bodies
Digestive	Mouth, esophagus, stomach, intestines, liver, and pancreas	Captures nutrients from ingested food
Urinary	Kidneys and bladder	Removes waste from bloodstream
Muscular	Skeletal, cardiac, and smooth muscle	Produces movement
Reproductive	Testes (male) and ovaries (female)	To reproduce
Integumentary	Skin, hair, nails, and sweat glands	Covers and protects the body
Excretory	Lungs, kidneys, and skin	Rids the body of toxins

Health and Safety

The primary functions, processes, and development

Human Growth and Development:

As teachers, we must understand the students' needs. Of course, there is no one rule for addressing the needs of all of our students, but it is important for us to know that they all have physical, social, and emotional needs. Each age group has its own needs, and, within each age group, there are differences between boys and girls to consider.

For years, we have utilized the wisdom of famed psychoanalyst Erik Erikson and his Eight Stages of Psychosocial Development Theory:

- Infant (birth to 1 year) – *Trust vs. Mistrust:* needs maximum comfort to feel safe in the world.
- Toddler (1 to 3 years) – *Autonomy vs. Shame and Doubt:* works to master his or her physical environment and become independent.
- Preschooler (3 to 6 years) – *Initiative vs. Guilt:* moves from initiation to trying new activities on their own and develops gender identity.
- School-Age Child (6 years to preadolescence) – *Industry vs. Inferiority:* learns to work with peers.
- Adolescent (adolescent years) – *Identity vs. Identity Confusion:* tries imitating different roles while developing a self-image, utilizing role models and contending with peer pressure.
- Young Adult (young adulthood) – *Intimacy vs. Isolation:* learns to make commitments to another person, such as a spouse, a parent, or a partner.
- Middle-Age Adult (middle adult) – *Generativity vs. Stagnation:* seeks satisfaction through productivity in career, family, and civic interests.
- Older Adult (late life) – *Integrity vs. Despair:* finds satisfaction in one's life accomplishments, deals with loss and preparation for death (Kail & Cavanaugh, 2010).

Health and Safety
The primary functions, processes, and development

The Basic Principles of Human Nutrition
- Students should be educated on how to select foods that contain proper nutrients.
- Students should be educated on how to read food labels.
- Students should be educated on how to follow dietary guidelines to promote healthy eating habits.
- Students should be educated on how to protect themselves from foodborne illnesses.

Health and Safety
Communicable and noncommunicable diseases and strategies for preventing or treating

Communicable Diseases – also known as an infectious disease. They are contagious and are spread or transmitted from person to person. Common communicable diseases in children are: flu, colds, chicken pox, respiratory infection, bronchitis, sinus infections, tonsil infections, and sexually transmitted diseases.

How to prevent infections/communicable diseases:
- Vaccination – introduces a small amount of the disease into the body and the body creates antibodies and is ready to defend itself.
- Hand Washing – washes away bacteria, germs, and infection that can enter the body.
- Exercise – keeps the body in good working order and builds a strong heart and lungs.
- Antibiotics – help us recover from bacterial infections.
  NOTE: antibiotics are powerless against viruses.

Non-Communicable Diseases – are diseases that are not contagious. These are caused by genetics, lifestyle, and/or environment. Examples include heart disease, cancer, diabetes, hypertension, and obesity.

Health and Safety
Characteristics of interpersonal relationships and healthy interpersonal relationships

Interpersonal Relationship – is a relationship between two or more people. It is important that our students have and maintain good relationships with their families and with their peers. As teachers, it is our job to not only teach the curriculum and standards, but it also falls upon us to foster our students' social and emotional health. There are six major areas of social and emotional growth. They include communication skills, self-concept, fair play, conflict resolution, stress management, and character development.

Communication Skills – Students should be advised that communication skills are important. There are three components that ensure students are communicating properly. These are eye contact, speaking clearly and correctly, and taking turns speaking, making sure not to interrupt and paying close attention for response and understanding.

Self-Concept – how our students see themselves. This is an important component of self-confidence.

Fair Play – treating everyone equally and with an impartial attitude. This is as important now as it was in the past. It is important to teach children that everyone should be treated the same and governed under the same rules.

Conflict Resolution – Teaching these skills can aid students in settling arguments on their own without always running to tell the teacher. Steps: first, stop before you get angry, this will allow the problem to be solved. Second, talk about the cause of the argument and decide what each participant wants. Third, think about your options. Fourth, choose a positive outcome for all. Finally, if no resolution is decided, ask an outsider for an opinion. Rules for conflict resolution: don't name-call, take turns talking, don't interrupt the speaker, be clear and honest about what is bothering you, listen, don't be violent, and be willing to compromise.

Stress Management – Just as adults can, our students can experience stress, and just like stress can do to us, it can get them in a funk. It is important to teach students the importance of asking questions when something is bothering them and talking about their problems or fears. Stress can also be reduced with physical exercise, eating right, and mental exercises such as deep breathing and meditation.

Health and Safety
Characteristics of interpersonal relationships and healthy interpersonal relationships

Character Development – Character is often defined as all the qualities that make people who they are. These include qualities like caring, citizenship, fairness, respect, responsibility, and trustworthiness.
According to the Josephson Institute, these qualities can be demonstrated in a number of ways. Teachers can create activates that help students develop their character.

- Caring – can be demonstrated by being kind, generous, grateful, compassionate, and helpful.
- Citizenship – can be demonstrated by volunteering, voting, and obeying laws, rules, and authority.
- Fairness – can be demonstrated by playing by the rules, sharing, and not taking advantage of classmates.
- Respect – can be demonstrated by using good manners, not hitting or threatening, and treating others how you would like to be treated.
- Responsibility – can be demonstrated by staying on task, being accountable, and setting an example for others.
- Trustworthiness – can be demonstrated by being honest, not cheating, being loyal, and being reliable (Josephson Institute, 2011).

Health and Safety

Strategies for maintaining personal emotional and physical health

Healthy Living:
Research has shown that when a person is physically active and takes care of themself, that person is physically healthy. There are a number of things students can learn in order to maintain their health. Below are suggestions for maintaining student health:

- Eating healthful food from diverse food groups for a healthy body.
- Utilizing proper safety procedures and equipment to protect themselves from injury. An example is wearing a helmet during sports, biking, and skating to prevent injury.
- Students should be advised to sleep an average of eight hours a day.
- Hand washing for disease prevention; proper hand washing should be taught from an early age.
- When spending time outdoors, students should be educated on protection from the sun. Education about sunscreen, long sleeves, and hats should be taught, especially in a state such as Florida.
- Students should be aware that emotional health is important and can affect how they feel. Students should be encouraged to talk about their feelings for healthy relationships.
- When exercising, students should be encouraged to warm up, workout and cool down.

Good health includes exercise as well as nutrition.

A nutritious diet consists of food from all of the basic food groups, including grains, meats, fruits, vegetables, dairy, and healthy fats. Grains should be in the form of whole grains. Meats or proteins should be in the form of lean meats and beans. A variety of fruits should be eaten in the form of fresh, frozen, or dried. Students should be advised to go easy on fruit juices because they contain additional sugar. Foods from the dairy group should be low-fat or fat-free. Foods from the vegetable group should be consumed in a wide variety.

Students should be advised that sodas and junk food are unhealthy and are full of empty calories, meaning they have no nutritional value. They should also be educated on the importance of taking vitamins and staying hydrated.

Health and Safety
Effects of substance abuse and factors contributing to substance abuse

Tobacco Products and Other Drugs:

Substance Abuse:
Warning Signs of Teen Drug Use – According to www.helpguide.org, a non-profit group for resolving health challenges, there are many warning signs of substance abuse in youth. Things a teacher may notice include, but are not limited to, the following:
- Skipping class
- New interest in drug-related fashions
- Avoiding eye contact
- Declining grades
- Getting into trouble at school
- Acting uncharacteristically isolated, withdrawn, or depressed

Symptoms of Substance Abuse:
- Smelling of alcohol, marijuana, or stale smoke
- Frequent minor illnesses, injuries, and infections
- Memory lapses
- Weight changes
- Frequent use of eye drops for bloodshot eyes

Prevention of Substance Abuse:
In most cases, the most promising prevention strategies have been programs that offer education about substance abuse.

Health and Safety

Questions to Recap:

1. What is the primary function of the immune system and the integumentary system?

2. In the _____ stage of Erikson's Psychosocial Development Theory, the person becomes independent.

3. In order to help a person be physically healthy, it is important that proper _____ is taught from an early age.

4. Qualities of character include all of the following except:
    a. Citizenship
    b. Cheating
    c. Respect
    d. Irresponsibility
    e. a and c
    f. a and d

1.) removes and filters out foreign bodies   2.) toddler   3.) nutrition   4.) e

Physical Education

Safety practices to avoid accidents and injuries

Safety and Well-Being:
Fire Safety – This is an important concept to cover with students. The process of 'stop, drop, and roll' is an important one, as well as what to do in case of a fire, such as installing smoke detectors, fire extinguishers, escape routes, and having a place.
Thunderstorm Safety – These are storms accompanied by heavy rain, lightning, and thunder. You should educate your students on what to do in case of a storm: stay inside, or, if outdoors, seek shelter in a low area or closed vehicle, and listen to the weather.
First Aid – Applications should be covered as well, such as what to do for choking and severe bleeding.

Students need to receive education about proper food preparation and hand washing skills as well.
Yearly Physicals, stretching and proper exercising.

Physical Education

Components of health-related fitness and activities for promoting each of the components

Physical Fitness – is the ability to perform physical activities while being energetic and alert. There are five components of physical fitness: cardiorespiratory endurance, muscular strength, muscular endurance, flexibility, and healthful body composition.
   Cardiorespiratory Endurance – is the ability of the cardiovascular and respiratory system to supply enough oxygen to the body during physical activity.
   Muscular Strength – is the amount of force a muscle can generate.
   Muscular Endurance – is the ability of a muscle to complete activities without getting tired.
   Flexibility – describes the range of motion of joints.
   Healthful Body Composition – describes a high ratio of lean muscle to fat.

Physical Education

Components of health-related fitness and activities for promoting each of the components

Exercise – is planned or structured, repetitive bodily movement that is done to maintain or improve physical fitness. There are five common types of exercise: aerobic, anaerobic, isometric, isotonic, and isokinetic.

- **Aerobic** – is an exercise that uses large amounts of oxygen for a long time. These types of exercise are vigorous and can either be continuous or rhythmic. This exercise type tends to improve endurance and strength.
- **Anaerobic** – is an exercise that uses high amounts of oxygen faster than the body can replenish it. Exercises include running sprints, tennis, or basketball.
- **Isometric** – is an exercise that involves the tightening of a body part for five to eight seconds. These can be done anywhere with no equipment and can raise blood pressure if the person holds their breath during the movements.
- **Isotonic** – is an exercise that involves using weights or resistance. Examples include weight lifting, pushups, and jumping jacks.
- **Isokinetic** – is an exercise that uses machines to isolate a muscle or muscle group.

Physical Education

Development of locomotor, nonlocomotor, manipulative, and perceptual awareness skills

Fundamental Motor Skills – are body movement skills that are required for students to be able to move through their environments. These are divided into three types: locomotor, nonlocomotor, and manipulative skills.

- **Locomotor Skill Development** – is used to move the body from one place to another and includes skills like walking, running, jumping, hopping, skipping, leaping, sliding, and galloping.
- **Nonlocomotor Skill Development** – is movement done while standing in place and includes skills like bending, stretching, pushing, pulling, balancing, twisting, and bouncing.
- **Manipulative Skills Development** – involves the handling of an object. These skills are found in many games and include throwing, striking, kicking, and catching.
- **Perceptual Motor Development** – is the ability to receive, interpret, and respond successfully to sensory tasks like drawing, building with blocks, and tossing and rolling a ball in a straight path in a game of kick ball.

Physical Education

Questions to Recap:

1. The process of 'stop, drop, and roll' is an important part of _____ safety.

2. Name three of the components of physical fitness.

3. Which of the following is not a type of exercise?
    a. Isometric
    b. Isokinetic
    c. Locomotor
    d. Aerobic

1.) fire 2.) cardiorespiratory endurance, muscular strength, muscular endurance, flexibility, healthful body composition 3.) c

The Arts

Elements, concepts, and terms associated with dance, music, drama, and the visual arts

Dance:
There are various styles of dance, such as cultural dance, modern dance, ballet, structured dance, and social dance.

Music:
Rhythm – is how the music moves through time; a general term. This word encompasses other terms such as beat, meter, and tempo. This is how fast or slow the music moves.
- Beat – the background pace of the music; students are taught to keep the beat by clapping their hands or by tapping their feet.
- Meter – describes how the beats are organized (1, 2, 3, 4).
- Tempo – describes how fast the music moves: slow, moderate, fast, or very fast.

Melody – pitches together in a sequence that forms a pattern.
Form – the pattern of repetition in music, such as AAA or ABC
Texture – the way a melody is used.
- Monophony – melody stands alone.
- Homophony – melody has accompaniment; this provides layers to the music, and it can portray, for example, a calm scene with impending doom lurking in the background.

Timbre – the distinct property of the piece, such as uplifting/high tones.
Dynamics – the volume of the music: soft, very soft, regular, somewhat loud, and very loud.

These can be used to convey meaning. For example, having your students listen to "Madame Butterfly," by Giacomo Puccini, allows them to hear the fast tempo and upbeat sound, and they may be inspired to draw a bright, busy picture.

Drama:
Acting – Students portray characters and communicate their lives.
Plot – is usually in the form of a script (character parts).
Perspective – is the viewpoint of the story.

The Arts

Elements, concepts, and terms associated with dance, music, drama, and the visual arts

Visual Arts:

Medium – is the product used to portray an image or meaning. It can be anything such as paper-maché, clay, ceramic, painting (watercolors), sculpture, and drawing.

Elements:
- Line – a mark with greater length than width
- Color – the light reflected off the object
- Shape – a chopped line
- Form – three-dimensional shapes
- Texture – the surface quality that can be seen

Principles:
- Balance – the distribution of object, color, and texture
- Movement – the path the viewer's eye takes (hallway)

The Arts

Arts and communication, self-expression, and social expression

In Music – Rhythm, melody, form, texture, and timbre can be used to convey meaning.

In Visual Art – Color, texture, and tone can be used to convey a mood or feeling in a painting or sculpture.

In Dance – Dance can portray emotion through body movements. An example is ballet.

The Arts
Connections among the arts and curriculum and everyday life

Art can be utilized in almost every area in the curriculum. This is an important tool that should be utilized. Art is a good source of differentiation. It is important to ensure that the students do not get lost in the art project and forget the concept the teacher is trying to enforce.

The arts are present in cultures and throughout history.

Art is often used to promote critical analysis, cultural perspectives, and aesthetic understandings of the arts.

Arts can be used to communicate, for self-expression, and social expression.

Questions to Recap:

1. _____ is how fast or slow music is and uses terms such as beat, _____, and _____ to describe it.

2. Movement and balance are _____ of the visual arts.

3. Self-expression in the arts can be conveyed in which of the following:
    a. In music, through melody and form
    b. In visual arts, through color and rhythm
    c. In dance, through body movements
    d. a and c
    e. All of the above

1.) rhythm, meter, tempo 2.) principles 3.) e

Extra Math Review Questions

Simplify the following expressions:

1.) $15x + 9 - 4 + 10$

2.) $(12 \times 3)x + 3x - 2$

3.) $15x + 5 + 2y - 3$

4.) $x + x(4 \times 3)$

5.) The reverse of multiplying by 7 is…

6.) The reverse of subtracting 27 is…

7.) The product of the length and width…

8.) Eight less than the number of puppies…

9.) Seven increased by the total of a number and two.

10.) Twelve decreased by the total of a number and seven yields 20.

11.) If 75 is added to 6 times some number, then the sum is 171. What is the number?

12.) My grandmother had a slight obsession with collecting fancy teacups. When she decided she had too many she kept ten for herself and divided the rest among her three daughters, and each on got 27. How many teacups did she have?

Extra Math Review Questions

Words in Math

13.) A single row team crew member can row at a rate of seven miles per hour in calm lack water. However this week's race it on the river, with the current the team member can row 18 miles per hour. How fast is the current of the river?

14.) We are going on a trip and taking Interstate 75 from south Georgia to Chattanooga TN, if we travel 463 miles at 75 miles per hour, how long will the trip take?
$Distance = rate \times time$

15.) A small private school has a maximum capacity of 480 students. Each classroom is designed for 20 students. How many classrooms are there?

16.) On a field trip to the aquarium students count 46 fish in a display. Seven of the fish are lion fish and thirteen of the fish are clownfish. The rest of the fish are pacific blue surgeonfish, how many of these are there?

17.) Round 2,342 to the nearest hundred.

18.) Round 3,585 to the nearest ten.

19.) Round 4,689 to the nearest thousand.

Greater than, less than, or equal to:

20.) 22 ( ) 65   **21.)** 23 × 2 ( ) 45   **22.)** 16 ( ) 256 ÷ 16

Extra Math Review Questions

Fractions

23.) Draw a chart that represents $\frac{3}{7}$.

24.) Shade in $\frac{1}{3}$

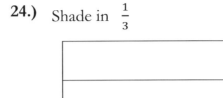

25.) Write the fraction for:

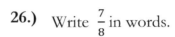

26.) Write $\frac{7}{8}$ in words.

27.) Write $\frac{5}{9}$ in words

28.) Convert $\frac{3}{8}$ to a percent

29.) Convert $\frac{3}{5}$ to a decimal

30.) $\frac{4}{7} + \frac{1}{7}$

31.) $\frac{7}{19} + \frac{11}{19}$

32.) Reduce $\frac{7}{49}$

33.) Reduce $\frac{12}{60}$

Extra Math Review Questions

Fractions

34.) $\dfrac{1}{3} \times \dfrac{5}{8}$

35.) $\dfrac{7}{11} \times \dfrac{3}{5}$

36.) $\dfrac{3}{5} \times \dfrac{12}{18}$

37.) $\dfrac{1}{5} + \dfrac{5}{8}$

38.) $\dfrac{1}{3} + \dfrac{3}{4}$

39.) $\dfrac{3}{10} + \dfrac{5}{12}$

40.) $\dfrac{1}{2} \div \dfrac{5}{8}$

41.) $\dfrac{2}{2} \div \dfrac{3}{4}$

42.) $\dfrac{3}{10} \div \dfrac{7}{12}$

43.) $\dfrac{2}{3} \times \dfrac{5}{11}$

44.) $-\dfrac{2}{3} \times -\dfrac{8}{15}$

45.) $\dfrac{11}{12} - \dfrac{3}{8} + \dfrac{5}{24}$

46.) $\dfrac{6}{6} \div \dfrac{3}{4}$

47.) $-\dfrac{16}{3} \div -\dfrac{3}{12}$

48.) $\dfrac{12}{15} + \dfrac{11}{30} - \dfrac{1}{45}$

49.) $(-0.0456) \div (-0.32)$

Extra Math Review Questions

Fractions

50.) -1.25×4.11 51.) $2.548 + 5.31$ 52.) $-45.92 - 5.26$

53.) $125.45 \div 4.5$ 54.) $241.2 - 2.2598$

Integers

55.) $|-27|$ 56.) $4 - |5 - 6|$ 57.) $|6 \times (2 - 7)|$

58.) $20 \div -2$ 59.) -5×11 60.) $14 \times (-2) \times (-2)$

61.) $-7 + 13$ 62.) $-22 - 19$ 63.) $-12 - (-13)$

64.) $-44 + (-41)$ 65.) $12 - |9 - 22|$ 66.) $12 - |-3 \times 2|$

Extra Math Review Questions

Integers

67.) $-2 \times (-11)$ **68.)** $-45 \div 3$ **69.)** $(3 \times (-12)) \div 2 + (-8)$

Solve

70.) $12 \times 4 - 36 \div 18$ **71.)** $12 \div 3 \times -(9 \div 3)$

72.) $[4 \times (5 + 7)] - (5 \times 4)$ **73.)** $[(-6 \times 2) + (-2 - 2)] \div (-4 \times (-1))$

Extra Math Review Questions

Solve

74.) $[(12 \times 2) - (-8 + 2)] \times (-10 \times 2)$

Geometry

75.) 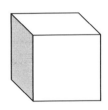 How many faces does a cube have?

How many edges does a cube have?

76.) 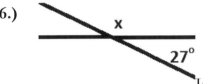 If angle x and the 27° are supplementary, what is the measure of x?

77.) Nixon wants to buy new carpet for his master bedroom that measures 12 feet by 18 feet. How many square yards of carpet will he have to buy?

78.) Using the results from problem 77, how much will the carpet cost if he find carpet that is $12 per square foot?

Extra Math Review Questions

Geometry

79.) Sharon is building a patio near her new pool, that has to go around the pool pump in an "L" shape, if the sides measure 10 feet, 11 feet, 4 feet, 5 feet, 5 feet, and 6 feet what is the perimeter of the patio?

80.) Sharon's new pool has a radius of 16 feet, what is the circumference of her pool?

81.) Find the volume for a cylinder that has the height of 20in and the diameter of 14in.

82.) Find the volume of a box that measures 8 in by 10 in, by 6 in on each side.

83.) What is the volume of a sphere with the radius of 5 in? (*hint* $V = \frac{4}{3}\pi r^3$)

Extra Math Review Questions

Solve using 5 for 'x' and 3 for 'y' in each of the expressions:

84.) $(x-2)+12$ 85.) $17-(15-x)$ 86.) $4x+6y$

87.) $3x+7$ 88.) $\dfrac{21}{y}+6$ 89.) $5(y-2)+45$

Solve

90.) $x+27=52$ 91.) $x-23=5$ 92.) $x+15=6$

93.) $x-5=-6$ 94.) $5+x=35$ 95.) $22=x+27$

96.) $-56=x-7$ 97.) $17=x-6$ 98.) $x+12>20$

Extra Math Review Questions

Solve

99.) $8x - 13 = 3$

100.) $-3x - 13 + (-3) = 11 + (-6)$

101.) Emily has two pea plants in her garden with 63 pea pods between them. One plant has 21 pods. How many pods are on the other plant?

102.) It is spring in Georgia so the high temperature for the day can occur at one a.m. If it is 37degree at 2p.m. and the temperature dropped 22degrees since. What was the temperature at one a.m.?

103.) Kim was watching a football game with her husband and the team did not seem to be making much progress towards the end zone. They ran for 6yds, then lost 7yds, the passed for 22 yards, only to be push back 11yds. Has the team made any progress towards a touchdown?

Extra Math Review Questions

Inequalities

104.) $x - 5 \leq 2$ **105.)** $x + 6 \geq -12$

106.) $x - (-8) < -15$ **107.)** $20 + x < -9$

108.) $25 > x - 5$ **109.)** $10 \geq x + 5$ **110.)** $27 - x \leq 13$

111.) Graph: $x - 3 \leq 1$ **112.)** Graph: $-3 \leq x + 3$

113.) Graph the following: the numbers greater than -4 but less than 2.

Extra Math Review Questions

Graphing

114.) The following ordered pair $(2, 1)$ is the solution for which of the following?

A) $-x + y = 3$

B) $2x - y = 3$

C) $-10x + 15y = 5$

115.) Graph the following points: $(2,3)$, $(0,1)$, and $(-2,-2)$.

116.) Find the slope of the line from 115. $slope \rightarrow$
$$m = \frac{y_2 - y_1}{x_2 - x_1}$$

Solve

117.) $15x = 45$

118.) $\frac{1}{4}x = 3$

119.) $-16x = 20$

120.) $\frac{1}{2}x = -3$

121.) $\frac{x}{9} = 27$

122.) $\frac{x}{-7} = 5$

Extra Math Review Questions

Solve

123.) $\dfrac{56}{x} = -8$

124.) $\dfrac{x}{5} = -\dfrac{10}{5}$

125.) $\dfrac{2x}{10} = \dfrac{4}{10}$

126.) $-5x \leq 25$

127.) $2x \leq \dfrac{3}{2}$

128.) $\dfrac{x}{3} > \dfrac{5}{3}$

129.) Nattily is about to compete in her first 10k run, if she runs 7km per hour the entire time, how long will it take her to finish.

130.) Todd swims every morning before school and wants to swim the shortest distance across the English Channel which is the Strait of Dover at 34 km. If he swims at 2km per hour how long will it take him to cross the channel?

Extra Math Review Questions

Solve

131.) For a wedding toast a bride will need enough Champaign for 200 guests if one bottle has 11 servings how many bottles does she need for her big day?

132.) $1 + 2^2$

133.) $8 \times 2^2 - 3^4$

134.) $(5-4)^{10} + (7-5)^3$

135.) 5^0

136.) $5^2 \times 5^3$

137.) $\left(\dfrac{1}{5}\right)^3$

138.) $4^5 \div 4^3$

139.) $(2^3)^3$

140.) $(4^3)^{-2}$

Extra Math Review Questions

Scientific Notation:

141.) 2.2×10^5

142.) 5.34×10^{-3}

143.) Write in scientific notation:
.000000159

144.) For my friend surprise baby shower we ordered two sheet cakes. One was chocolate with chocolate icing and the other was yellow cake with whipped cream icing. After the shower there were only 8 out of 32 piece of chocolate left and 4 out of 16 left. Are the two portions of left over cake an equal proportion?

145.) The local church is selling raffle tickets for a house donated by well-known philanthropist. The tickets are $100 each, however they are only selling 1000 tickets. What are your odds of winning if you bought 5 tickets?

146.) Clair passed all of her class. She made a 89 in geometry, 91 in chemistry, 99 in band, 75 in English Lit., 82 in Government, and a 78 in Home Economics. What was her mean, median, and range?

147.) Bill rented a moving van for $19 per day and drove 1200 miles over a 5 day period. The rental company allotted him 150 free miles per day, though there is a charge of $0.25 for each additional mile. What was the total rental cost?

Extra Math Review Questions

Solve

148.) In the table below customers can find the cost per ounce of a certain type of caviar. What is the cost of five ounces?

Caviar (ounces)	Cost (dollars)
1	10.32
2	12.64
3	4.96
4	17.28
5	19.60
6	21.92
7	24.24

149.) Using the information provided in the table, regarding the age of southern yellow pine tree and the diameter or width of the tree trunk. How old is a pine tree that is 11 inches in diameter?

Trunk Diameter (inches)	Age (years)
4	2
5	4
6	6
7	8
8	10
9	12

150.) In a flock of Canadian Geese there are 72 members with 12 males. How many females are there?

Math Review Answers

1.) $15x + 9 - 4 + 10$

$15x + 9 - 4 + 10$

$15x + 5 + 10$

$15x + 15$ or

$15(x + 1)$

2.) $(12 \times 3)x + 3x - 2$

$(12 \times 3)x + 3x - 2$

$(36)x + 3x - 2$

$39x - 2$

3.) $15x + 5 + 2y - 3$

$15x + 5 + 2y - 3$

$15x + 2y + 2$

4.) $x + x(4 \times 3)$

$x + x(4 \times 3)$

$x + x(12)$

$13x$

5.) The reverse of multiplying by 7 is..

$\div 7$

6.) The reverse of subtracting 27 is…

$+27$

7.) The product of the length and width

$l \times w$

8.) Eight less than the number of puppies

$puppies - 8$

9.) Seven increased by the total of a number and two

$(x + 2) + 7$

10.) Twelve decreased by the total of a number and seven yields 20

$(x + 7) - 12 = 20$

Math Review Answers

11.) If 75 is added to 6 times some number, then the sum is 171. What is the number?

$$(6 \times x) + 75 = 171$$
$$6x + 75 = 171$$
$$\underline{-75 \quad -75}$$
$$\frac{6x = 96}{6 \quad \quad 6}$$
$$x = 16$$

12.) My grandmother had a slight obsession with collecting fancy teacups. When she decided she had too many she kept ten for herself and divided the rest among her three daughters, and each on got 27. How many teacups did she have?

$$(27 \times 3) + 10$$
$$(81) + 10$$
$$91$$

13.) A single row team crew member can row at a rate of seven miles per hour in calm lack water. However this week's race it on the river, with the current the team member can row 18 miles per hour. How fast is the current of the river?

$$18mph - 7mph =$$
$$11mph \; current$$

14.) We are going on a trip and taking Interstate 75 from south Georgia to Chattanooga TN, if we travel 463 miles at 75 miles per hour, how long will the trip take? **Distance = rate × time**

$$D = r \times t$$
$$\frac{463 = 75t}{75 \quad \quad 75}$$
$$6.173 = t$$

Math Review Answers

15.) A small private school has a maximum capacity of 480 students. Each classroom is designed for 20 students. How many classrooms are there?

$$\frac{480}{20} = 24 \; classrooms$$

16.) On a field trip to the aquarium students count 46 fish in a display. Seven of the fish are lion fish and thirteen of the fish are clownfish. The rest of the fish are pacific blue surgeonfish, how many of these are there?

$$46 = 7 + 13 + x$$
$$46 = 20 + x$$
$$\underline{20 - 20}$$
$$-26 = x$$

17.) Round 2,342 to the nearest hundred.

2,300

18.) Round 3,585 to the nearest ten.

3,590

19.) Round 4,689 to the nearest thousand.

5,000

20.) 22 ( ) 65

<

21.) 23 × 2 ( ) 45

>

22.) 16 ( ) 256 ÷ 16

=

23.) Draw a chart that represents $\frac{3}{7}$.

24.) Shade in $\frac{1}{3}$

Math Review Answers

25.) Write the fraction for:

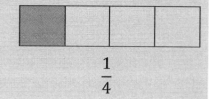

$\frac{1}{4}$

26.) Write $\frac{7}{8}$ in words.

Seven-eighths

27.) Write $\frac{5}{9}$ in words

Five-ninths

28.) Convert $\frac{3}{8}$ to a percent

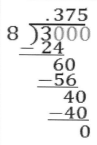

To convert .375 to a percent move the decimal two places to the right and attach a percent sign. 0.375 = 37.5%

29.) Convert $\frac{3}{5}$ to a decimal

$$5 \overline{)\begin{array}{r} .6 \\ 30 \\ -30 \\ \hline 0 \end{array}}$$

30.) $\frac{4}{7} + \frac{1}{7}$

$\frac{5}{7}$

31.) $\frac{7}{19} + \frac{11}{19}$

$\frac{18}{19}$

32.) Reduce $\frac{7}{49}$

$\frac{1}{7}$

33.) Reduce $\frac{12}{60}$

$\frac{1}{5}$

Math Review Answers

34.) $\dfrac{1}{3} \times \dfrac{5}{8}$

$\dfrac{1}{3} \times \dfrac{5}{8} = \dfrac{5}{24}$

35.) $\dfrac{7}{11} \times \dfrac{3}{5}$

$\dfrac{7}{11} \times \dfrac{3}{5} = \dfrac{21}{55}$

36.) $\dfrac{3}{5} \times \dfrac{12}{18}$

$\dfrac{3}{5} \times \dfrac{12}{18} = \dfrac{36}{90} = \dfrac{2}{5}$

37.) $\dfrac{1}{5} + \dfrac{5}{8}$

$\dfrac{(8)1}{(8)5} + \dfrac{5(5)}{8(5)} =$

$\dfrac{8}{40} + \dfrac{25}{40} = \dfrac{33}{40}$

38.) $\dfrac{1}{3} + \dfrac{3}{4}$

$\dfrac{(4)1}{(4)3} + \dfrac{3(3)}{4(3)}$

$= \dfrac{4}{12} + \dfrac{9}{12}$

$= \dfrac{13}{12} \text{ or } 1\dfrac{1}{12}$

39.) $\dfrac{3}{10} + \dfrac{5}{12}$

$\dfrac{(6)3}{(6)10} + \dfrac{5(5)}{12(5)} =$

$\dfrac{18}{60} + \dfrac{25}{60} = \dfrac{43}{60}$

40.) $\dfrac{1}{2} \div \dfrac{5}{8}$

$\dfrac{1}{2} \div \dfrac{5}{8} = \dfrac{1}{2} \times \dfrac{8}{5} =$

$\dfrac{8}{10} \text{ or } \dfrac{4}{5}$

41.) $\dfrac{2}{2} \div \dfrac{3}{4}$

$\dfrac{2}{2} \div \dfrac{3}{4} = \dfrac{2}{2} \times \dfrac{4}{3} = \dfrac{8}{6} \text{ or } \dfrac{4}{3} \text{ or } 1\dfrac{1}{3}$

Math Review Answers

42.) $\dfrac{3}{10} \div \dfrac{7}{12}$

$\dfrac{3}{10} \div \dfrac{7}{12} = \dfrac{3}{10} \times \dfrac{12}{7} =$

$\dfrac{36}{70} \text{ or } \dfrac{18}{35}$

43.) $\dfrac{2}{3} \times \dfrac{5}{11}$

$\dfrac{2}{3} \times \dfrac{5}{11} = \dfrac{10}{33}$

44.) $-\dfrac{2}{3} \times -\dfrac{8}{15}$

$-\dfrac{2}{3} \times -\dfrac{8}{15} = \dfrac{16}{45}$

45.) $\dfrac{11}{12} - \dfrac{3}{8} + \dfrac{5}{24}$

$\dfrac{11}{12} - \dfrac{3}{8} + \dfrac{5}{24} =$

$\dfrac{(2)11}{(2)12} - \dfrac{(3)3}{(3)8} + \dfrac{5}{24} =$

$\dfrac{22}{24} - \dfrac{9}{24} + \dfrac{5}{24} =$

$\dfrac{13}{24} + \dfrac{5}{24} = \dfrac{6}{8} = \dfrac{3}{4}$

46.) $\dfrac{6}{6} \div \dfrac{3}{4}$

$\dfrac{6}{6} \div \dfrac{3}{4} = \dfrac{6}{6} \times \dfrac{4}{3} =$

$\dfrac{24}{18} \text{ or } \dfrac{4}{3} = 1\dfrac{1}{3}$

47.) $-\dfrac{16}{3} \div -\dfrac{3}{12}$

$-\dfrac{16}{3} \div -\dfrac{3}{12} =$

$-\dfrac{16}{3} \times -\dfrac{12}{3} =$

$\dfrac{192}{3} = 64$

Math Review Answers

48.) $\dfrac{12}{15} + \dfrac{11}{30} - \dfrac{1}{45}$

$\dfrac{12}{15} + \dfrac{11}{30} - \dfrac{1}{45}$

$\dfrac{(6)12}{(6)15} + \dfrac{(3)11}{(3)30} - \dfrac{(2)1}{(2)45} =$

$\dfrac{72}{90} + \dfrac{33}{90} - \dfrac{2}{90} =$

$\dfrac{105}{90} - \dfrac{2}{90} = \dfrac{103}{90}$

49.) $(-0.0456) \div (-0.32)$

$0.32\overline{)0.0456}$ *Move denominator decimal to create whole number then do the same in the numerator*

```
        .1425
   32 )4.5600
      -3 2
       1 36
      -1 28
          80
         -64
         160
        -160
           0
```

50.) -1.25×4.11

-1.25×4.11

1.25×4.11
(drop negative to do the work)

```
      1 2
      1.25
    × 4.11
      1 25
     1250
   +50000
    5.1375
```

there are four decimal places in the original problem so count four places and add the decimal.

51.) $2.548 + 5.31$

```
   2.548
  +5.310
   7.858
```

52.) $-45.92 - 5.26$

```
     11
   -45.92
   - 5.26
   -51.18
```

Math Review Answers

53.) $125.45 \div 4.5$

$125.45 \div 4.5$

$45 \overline{)1254.5}$ *Move denominator decimal to create whole number then move the same number of spaces in the numerator*

$$\begin{array}{r} 27.877... \\ 45 \overline{)1254.500} \\ \underline{-90} \\ 354 \\ \underline{-315} \\ 395 \\ \underline{-360} \\ 350 \\ \underline{-315} \\ 350 \\ \underline{-315} \\ 35 \end{array}$$

54.) $241.2 - 2.2598$

$$\begin{array}{r} 241.2000 \\ -2.2598 \\ \hline 238.9402 \end{array}$$

55.) $|-27|$

27

56.) $4 - |5 - 6|$

$4 - |5 - 6|$

$4 - |-1|$

$4 - 1$

3

57.) $|6 \times (2 - 7)|$

$|6 \times (2 - 7)|$

$|6 \times (-5)|$

$|6 \times -5|$

$|-30|$

30

58.) $20 \div -2$

$20 \div -2$

-10

59.) -5×11

-5×11

-55

60.) $14 \times (-2) \times (-2)$

$14 \times (-2) \times (-2)$

$(-28) \times (-2)$

56

Math Review Answers

61.) $-7 + 13$

$-7 + 13$

6

62.) $-22 - 19$

$-22 - 19$

-41

63.) $-12 - (-13)$

$-12 - (-13)$

$-12 + 13$

1

64.) $-44 + (-41)$

$-44 + (-41)$

$-44 - 41$

-85

65.) $12 - |9 - 22|$

$12 - |9 - 22|$

$12 - |-13|$

$12 - 13$

-1

66.) $12 - |-3 \times 2|$

$12 - |-6|$

$12 - 6$

6

67.) $-2 \times (-11)$

$-2 \times (-11)$

22

68.) $-45 \div 3$

$-45 \div 3$

-15

69.) $(3 \times (-12)) \div 2 + (-8)$

$(3 \times (-12)) \div 2 + (-8)$

$(-36) \div 2 + (-8)$

$-18 + (-8)$

-26

70.) $12 \times 4 - 36 \div 18$

$12 \times 4 - 36 \div 18$

$48 - 2$

46

71.) $12 \div 3 \times -(9 \div 3)$

$12 \div 3 \times -(9 \div 3)$

$4 \times -(3)$

$4 \times (-3)$

-12

Math Review Answers

72.) $[4 \times (5 + 7)] - (5 \times 4)$

$[4 \times (5 + 7)] - (5 \times 4)$

$[4 \times (5 + 7)] - (20)$

$[4 \times (12)] - (20)$

$[48] - (20)$

28

73.) $[(-6 \times 2) + (-2 - 2)] \div (-4 \times (-1))$

$[(-6 \times 2) + (-2 - 2)] \div (-4 \times (-1))$

$[(-12) + (-2 - 2)] \div (-4 \times (-1))$

$[(-12) + (-4)] \div (-4 \times (-1))$

$[-16] \div (4)$

-4

74.) $[(12 \times 2) - (-8 + 2)] \times (-10 \times 2)$

$[(12 \times 2) - (-8 + 2)] \times (-10 \times 2)$

$[(24) - (-8 + 2)] \times (-10 \times 2)$

$[(24) - (-6)] \times (-10 \times 2)$

$[(24) - (-6)] \times (-20)$

$[30] \times (-20)$

-600

75.) How many faces does a cube have?

How many edges does a cube have?

6 faces, 12 edges

76.) If angle x and the 27° are supplementary, what is the measure of x?

X = 153°

Math Review Answers

77.) Nixon wants to buy new carpet for his master bedroom that measures 12 feet by 18 feet. How many square yards of carpet will he have to buy?

$$12ft \times 18ft = 216 sqft$$

so there are **9** sqft in **1** square yard and there are **24** sqyds in **216** sqft

78.) Using the results from problem ##, how much will the carpet cost if he find carpet that is $12 per square foot?

$$24 \times \$12 = \$288$$

79.) Sharon is building a patio near her new pool, that has to go around the pool pump in an "L" shape, if the sides measure 10 feet, 11 feet, 4 feet, 5 feet, 5 feet, and 6 feet what is the perimeter of the patio?

$$10 + 11 + 4 + 5 + 5 + 6 = 41 ft$$

80.) Sharon's new pool has a radius of 16 feet, what is the circumference of her pool?

$$C = 2\pi r$$
$$C = 2\pi 16$$
$$C = \pi 32$$
$$C = 100.8 ft$$

Math Review Answers

81.) Find the volume for a cylinder that has the height of 20in and the diameter of 14in.

$$V = \pi r^2 h$$
$$V = \pi 7^2 14$$
$$V = \pi(49)(14)$$
$$V = \pi(686)$$
$$V = 2160.9 in^3$$

82.) Find the volume of a box that measures 8 in by 10 in, by 6 in on each side.

$$V = blh$$
$$V = (8)(10)(6)$$
$$V = (80)(6)$$
$$V = 480 in^3$$

83.) What is the volume of a sphere with the radius of 5 in? (hint $V = \frac{4}{3} \pi r^3$)

$$V = \frac{4}{3} \pi r^3$$
$$V = \frac{4}{3} \pi 5^3$$
$$V = \frac{4}{3} \pi (125)$$
$$V = 523.6875 in^3$$

84.)
$(x - 2) + 12$
$(x - 2) + 12$
$(5 - 2) + 12$
$(3) + 12$
15

85.)
$17 - (15 - x)$
$17 - (15 - x)$
$17 - (15 - 5)$
$17 - (10)$
7

86.)
$4x + 6y$
$4x + 6y$
$4(5) + 6(3)$
$20 + 18$
38

87.)
$3x + 7$

$3x + 7$
$3(5) + 7$
$15 + 7$
22

88.)
$\frac{21}{y} + 6$
$\frac{21}{y} + 6$
$\frac{21}{3} + 6$
$7 + 6$
13

89.)
$5(y - 2) + 45$

$5(y - 2) + 45$
$5(3 - 2) + 45$
$5(1) + 45$
$5 + 45$
50

Math Review Answers

Solving Equations

90.) $x + 27 = 52$
$x + 27 = 52$
$\underline{-27 \quad -27}$
$x = 25$

91.) $x - 23 = 5$
$x - 23 = 5$
$\underline{+23 + 23}$
$x = 28$

92.) $x + 15 = 6$
$x + 15 = 6$
$\underline{-15 - 15}$
$x = -9$

93.) $x - 5 = -6$
$x - 5 = -6$
$\underline{+5 \quad +5}$
$x = -1$

94.) $5 + x = 35$
$5 + x = 35$
$\underline{-5 \quad -5}$
$x = 30$

95.) $22 = x + 27$
$22 = x + 27$
$\underline{-27 \quad -27}$
$-5 = x$

96.) $-56 = x - 7$
$-56 = x - 7$
$\underline{+7 \quad +7}$
$-49 = x$

97.) $17 = x - 6$
$17 = x - 6$
$\underline{+6}$
$\underline{+6}$
$23 = x$

98.) $x + 12 > 20$
$x + 12 > 20$
$\underline{-12 - 12}$
$x > 8$

99.) $8x - 13 = 3$
$8x - 13 = 3$
$\underline{+13 +13}$
$\underline{8x = 16}$
$8 \quad 8$
$x = 2$

100.) $-3x - 13 + (-3) = 11 + (-6)$
$-3x - 13 + (-3) = 11 + (-6)$
$-3x - 16 = 11 + (-6)$
$-3x - 16 = 5$
$\underline{+16 + 16}$
$\underline{-3x = 21}$
$-3 \quad -3$
$x = -7$

Math Review Answers

101.) Emily has two pea plants in her garden with 63 pea pods between them. One plant has 21 pods. How many pods are on the other plant?

$$x + 21 = 63$$
$$\underline{-21 \;\; -21}$$
$$x = 42$$

102.) It is spring in Georgia so the high temperature for the day can occur at one a.m. If it is 37degree at 2p.m. and the temperature dropped 22degrees since. What was the temperature at one a.m.?

$$37 \; 2p.m.$$
$$\underline{+22 \quad\quad}$$
$$59 \; at \; 1a.m.$$

103.) Kim was watching a football game with her husband and the team did not seem to be making much progress towards the end zone. They ran for 6yds, then lost 7yds, the passed for 22 yards, only to be push back 11yds. Has the team made any progress towards a touchdown?

$$6 - 11 + 21 - 11$$
$$= 10 yds$$

104.) $x - 5 \leq 2$

$$x - 5 \leq 2$$
$$\underline{+5 \; +5}$$
$$x \leq 7$$

105.) $x + 6 \geq -12$

$$x + 6 \geq -12$$
$$\underline{-6 \quad\; -6}$$
$$x \geq -18$$

Math Review Answers

106.) $x - (-8) < -15$

$x - (-8) < -15$
$x + 8 < -15$
$\underline{-8 -8}$
$x < -23$

107.) $20 + x < -9$

$20 + x < -9$
$\underline{-20 -20}$
$x < -29$

108.) $25 > x - 5$

$25 > x - 5$
$\underline{+5 +5}$
$30 > x$

109.) $10 \geq x + 5$

$10 \geq x + 5$
$\underline{-5}$
$\underline{-5}$
$5 \geq x$

110.) $27 - x \leq 13$

$27 - x \leq 13$
$\underline{-27 -27}$
$\underline{-x \leq -14}$
$-1 -1$
$x \geq 14$

111.) Graph: $x - 3 \leq 1$

$x - 3 \leq 1$
$\underline{+3 \ +3}$
$x \leq 4$

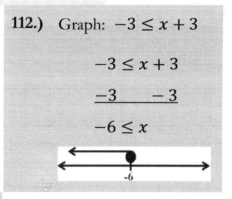

112.) Graph: $-3 \leq x + 3$

$-3 \leq x + 3$
$\underline{-3 -3}$
$-6 \leq x$

113.) Graph the following: the numbers greater than -4 but less than 2.

Math Review Answers

114.) The following ordered pair $(2, 1)$ is the solution for which of the following?
A) $-x + y = 3$
B) $2x - y = 3$
C) $-10x + 15y = 5$

B)
$2x - y = 3$
$2(2) - 1 = 3$
$4 - 1 = 3$
$3 = 3$

A)
$-x + y = 3$
$-x + y = 3$
$-2 + 1 = 3$
$-1 \neq 3$

C)
$-10x + 15y = 5$
$-10(2) + 15(1) = 5$
$-20 + 15 = 5$
$-5 \neq 5$

115.) Graph the following points: (2,3), (0,1), and (-2,-2).

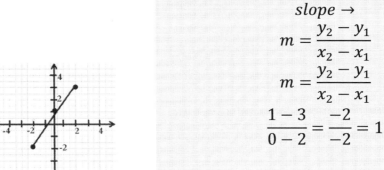

116.) Find the slope of the line from 115.

$$slope \rightarrow$$
$$m = \frac{y_2 - y_1}{x_2 - x_1}$$
$$m = \frac{y_2 - y_1}{x_2 - x_1}$$
$$\frac{1 - 3}{0 - 2} = \frac{-2}{-2} = 1$$

117.) $15x = 45$

$\dfrac{\cancel{15}x}{\cancel{15}} = \dfrac{45}{15}$

$x = 3$

118.) $\dfrac{1}{4}x = 3$

$\dfrac{\cancel{(4)}1}{4}x = 3(4)$

$1x = 3(4)$

$x = 12$

119.) $-16x = 20$

$\dfrac{\cancel{-16}x}{\cancel{-16}} = \dfrac{20}{-16}$

$x = 1\dfrac{1}{4}$

Math Review Answers

120.)
$$\frac{1}{2}x = -3$$
$$\frac{(2)1}{\cancel{2}}x = -3(2)$$
$$1x = -3(2)$$
$$x = -6$$

121.)
$$\frac{x}{9} = 27$$
$$\frac{(9)x}{\cancel{9}} = 27(9)$$
$$1x = 27(9)$$
$$x = 243$$

122.)
$$\frac{x}{-7} = 5$$
$$\frac{(-7)x}{\cancel{-7}} = 5(-7)$$
$$1x = 5(-7)$$
$$x = -35$$

123.)
$$\frac{56}{x} = -8$$
$$\frac{(\cancel{x})56}{\cancel{x}} = -8(x)$$
$$\frac{56 = -8(x)}{-8 \quad -8}$$
$$-7 = x$$

124.)
$$\frac{x}{5} = -\frac{10}{5}$$
$$\frac{(\cancel{5})x}{\cancel{5}} = -\frac{10(\cancel{5})}{\cancel{5}}$$
$$x = -10$$

125.)
$$\frac{2x}{10} = \frac{4}{10}$$
$$\frac{(\cancel{10})2x}{\cancel{10}} = -\frac{4(\cancel{10})}{\cancel{10}}$$
$$\frac{2x = -4}{2 \quad\quad 2}$$
$$x = -2$$

126.)
$$-5x \leq 25$$
$$\frac{-5x \leq 25}{-5 \quad -5}$$
$$x \geq -5$$

Math Review Answers

127.)

$$2x \leq \frac{3}{2}$$

$$2x \leq \frac{3}{2}$$

$$(2)2x \leq \frac{3\cancel{(2)}}{\cancel{2}}$$

$$\frac{4x \leq 3}{4 \quad 4}$$

$$x \leq \frac{3}{4}$$

128.)

$$\frac{x}{3} > \frac{5}{3}$$

$$\frac{x}{3} > \frac{5}{3}$$

$$\frac{\cancel{(3)}x}{\cancel{3}} > \frac{5\cancel{(3)}}{\cancel{3}}$$

$$x > 5$$

129.) Nattily is about to compete in her first 10k run, if she runs 7km per hour the entire time, how long will it take her to finish.

$$D = r \times t$$
$$10k = 7km \times t$$
$$\frac{10}{7} = t$$
$$1.42 = t$$

130.) Todd swims every morning before school and wants to swim the shortest distance across the English Channel which is the Strait of Dover at 34 km. If he swims at 2km per hour how long will it take him to cross the channel?

$$D = r \times t$$
$$34 = 2 \times t$$
$$\frac{34 = \cancel{2}t}{2 \quad \cancel{2}}$$
$$16 = t$$

Math Review Answers

131.) For a wedding toast a bride will need enough Champaign for 200 guests if one bottle has 11 servings how many bottles does she need for her big day?

$$\frac{200}{11} \text{ guests}$$

18.1, so 19 bottles

132.) $1 + 2^2$

$1 + 2^2$

$1 + 2 \times 2$

$1 + 4$

5

133.) $8 \times 2^2 - 3^4$

$8 \times 2^2 - 3^4$

$8 \times 2 \times 2 - 3 \times 3 \times 3 \times 3$

$8 \times 4 - 9 \times 9$

$32 - 81$

-49

134.) $(5-4)^{10} + (7-5)^3$

$(5-4)^{10} + (7-5)^3$

$(1)^{10} + (2)^3$

$1 + 2 \times 2 \times 2$

$1 + 4 \times 2$

$1 + 8$

9

135.) 5^0

5^0

1

136.) $5^2 \times 5^3$

$5^2 \times 5^3$

$(5 \times 5) \times (5 \times 5 \times 5)$

$(25) \times (125)$

3125

137.) $(\frac{1}{5})^3$

$(\frac{1}{5})^3$

$\frac{1}{5} \times \frac{1}{5} \times \frac{1}{5}$

$\frac{1}{25} \times \frac{1}{5}$

$\frac{1}{125}$

Math Review Answers

138.) $4^5 \div 4^3$

$4^5 \div 4^3$

$\dfrac{4 \times 4 \times \cancel{4} \times \cancel{4} \times \cancel{4}}{\cancel{4} \times \cancel{4} \times \cancel{4}}$

$4 \times 4 = 16$

139.) $(2^3)^3$

$(2^3)^3$

$(2 \times 2 \times 2)^3$

$(2 \times 2 \times 2)^3$

$(4 \times 2)^3$

$(8)^3$

$8 \times 8 \times 8$

64×8

512

140.) $(4^3)^{-2}$

$(4^3)^{-2}$

$(4 \times 4 \times 4)^{-2}$

$(16 \times 4)^{-2}$

$(64)^{-2}$

$\dfrac{1}{64 \times 64}$

$\dfrac{1}{4096}$

141.) 2.2×10^5

2.2×10^5

$220{,}000$

142.) 5.34×10^{-3}

5.34×10^{-3}

$.00534$

143.) Write in scientific notation:

$.000000159$

$.000000159$

$.000000159$

1.59×10^{-7}

Math Review Answers

144.) For my friend surprise baby shower we ordered two sheet cakes. One was chocolate with chocolate icing and the other was yellow cake with whipped cream icing. After the shower there were only 8 out of 32 piece of chocolate left and 4 out of 16 left. Are the two portions of left over cake an equal proportion?

$$\frac{8}{32} \rightarrow \frac{4}{16}$$

Cross multiply

$16 \times 8 = 128 \; or \; 32 \times 4 = 128$

so the proportions are equal

145.) The local church is selling raffle tickets for a house donated by well-known philanthropist. The tickets are $100 each, however they are only selling 1000 tickets. What are your odds of winning if you bought 5 tickets?

$$\frac{5}{1000} = \frac{1}{200}$$

146.) Clair passed all of her class. She made a 89 in geometry, 91 in chemistry, 99 in band, 75 in English Lit., 82 in Government, and a 78 in Home Economics. What was her mean, median, and range?

$$99 + 91 + 89 + 82 + 78 + 75$$

$$190 + 171 + 153$$

$$361 + 153$$

$$514$$

$$Mean \rightarrow \frac{514}{6} = 85.67$$

$$Median \rightarrow \frac{171}{2} = 85.5$$

$$Range \rightarrow 99 - 75$$

Math Review Answers

147.) Bill rented a moving van for $19 per day and drove 1200 miles over a 5 day period. The rental company allotted him 150 free miles per day, though there is a charge of $0.25 for each additional mile. What was the total rental cost?

$$5 \overline{)1200} = 240$$

Van $19 per day for 5 days
Five days divided by 1,200 miles. 240 minus the 150 per day allotment. Equals 90 miles per day for 5 days $(90 \times 5) .25 \rightarrow (450).25$----

$112.50 + $95 = $207.50 so the total cost of the car rental for 5 days is $207.50.

148.) In the table below customers can find the cost per ounce of a certain type of caviar. What is the cost of five ounces?

Caviar (ounces)	Cost (dollars)
1	10.32
2	12.64
3	□4.96
4	17.28
5	19.60
6	21.92
7	24.24

19.60

149.) Using the information provided in the table, regarding the age of southern yellow pine tree and the diameter or width of the tree trunk. How old is a pine tree that is 11 inches in diameter?

Trunk Diameter (inches)	Age (years)
4	2
5	4
6	6
7	8
8	10
9	12

10 inches = 14 years
12 inches = 16 years

150.) In a flock of Canadian Geese there are 72 members with 12 males. How many females are there?

$$72 = 12 + x$$
$$-12 - 12$$
$$60 = x \text{ or females}$$

References

Daniel, Lucy, Edward Paul Ortleb, and Alton Biggs. *Glencoe life science.* New York, N.Y.: Glencoe, 1997. Print.

Danzer, Gerald A. *The Americans reconstruction through the 20th century.* Evanston, IL: McDougal Littell/Houghton Mifflin, 1999. Print.

Duiker, William J., and Jackson J. Spielvogel. *The essential world history.* 3rd ed. Belmont, CA: Thomson Wadsworth, 2008. Print.

Early Childhood Education Preparation Guide. (2007, January 1). *Georgia Assessments for the Certification of Educators Preparation Guide.* Retrieved January 12, 2011, from www.gace.nesinc.com/PDFs/GA_PG_fld001002_complete.pdf.

Ellis, Elisabeth Gaynor, Anthony Esler, and Burton F. Beers. *Prentice Hall world history: connections to today.* Upper Saddle River, N.J.: Prentice Hall, 2001. Print.

Farah, Mounir, and Andrea Berens Karls. *World history the human experience.* New York, N.Y.: Glencoe/McGraw-Hill, 2001. Print.

Gay, K. Elayn. *Prealgebra.* 5th ed. Upper Saddle River, N.J.: Pearson Prentice Hall, 2008. Print.

Greata, Joanne. *An introduction to music in early childhood education.* Clifton Park, NY : Thomson Delmar Learning, 2006. Print.

Gunning, Thomas G. *Creating literacy instruction for all students.* 5th ed. Boston, MA: Allyn and Bacon, 2005. Print.

Hendrick, Joanne. *The whole child: developmental education for the early years.* 7th ed. Upper Saddle River, N.J.: Merrill, 2001. Print.

Hewitt, Paul G., John Suchocki, and Leslie A. Hewitt. *Conceptual physical science.* 3rd ed. San Francisco: Pearson / Addison Wesley, 2004. Print.

"Illustrated Mathematics Dictionary." *Math is Fun - Maths Resources.* Math is Fun, 1 Jan. 2010. Web. 21 Feb. 2011. <http://www.mathsisfun.com/definitions/>.

Johnson, George B., and Peter H. Raven. *Biology: principles & explorations.* Austin, [Tex.: Holt, Rinehart and Winston, 2001. Print.

Johnson, George Brooks, Jonathan B. Losos, William C. Ober, and Claire W. Garrison. *Essentials of the living world.* 2nd ed. Boston: McGraw-Hill, 2008. Print.

Kail, Robert V., Christine A. Ateah, and John C. Cavanaugh. *Human development: a life-span view.* Toronto: Thomson Nelson, 2006. Print.

Martin, Ralph E. *Teaching science for all children: an inquiry approach*. 4th ed. Boston: Pearson/Allyn and Bacon, 2005. Print.

"Math League Help Topics." *Math League*. Math League Press, 1 May 2006. Web. 21 Feb. 2011. <http://www.mathleague.com/help/help.htm>.

McLaughlin, Charles W., and Marilyn Thompson. *Glencoe physical science*. New York, N.Y.: Glencoe, 1999. Print.

Miller, Charles David, Vern E. Heeren, and E. John Hornsby. *Mathematical ideas*. 11th ed., expanded ed. Boston: Pearson Addison-Wesley, 2007. Print.

Padilla, Michael J., Ioannis Miaoulis, Martha Cyr, and Jan Jenner. *Earth science*. Boston, Mass.: Pearson Prentice Hall, 2009. Print.

Parker, Walter. *Social studies in elementary education*. 11th ed. Upper Saddle River, N.J.: Merrill, 2001. Print.

Sager, Robert J., and David M. Helgren. *World geography today*. Annotated teacher's ed. Austin: Holt, Rinehart, and Winston, 2000. Print.

Tompkins, Gail E. *Language arts: patterns of practice*. Upper Saddle River, N.J.: Pearson/Merrill/Prentice Hall, 2005. Print.

Walle, John A. *Elementary and middle school mathematics: teaching developmentally*. 4th ed. New York: Addison Wesley Longman, 2000. Print.

Webb, Frances Sizer, Eleanor Noss Whitney, and Linda K. DeBruyne. *Health: making life choices*. 2nd ed. Lincolnwood, Ill.: National Textbook Co., 2000. Print.

Made in the USA
Lexington, KY
25 February 2012